studysync®

Reading & Writing Companion

Testing Our Limits

What do we do when life gets hard?

studysync®

studysync.com

ISBN 978-1-94-469573-6

4 5 6 LMN 24 23 22 21 20

B

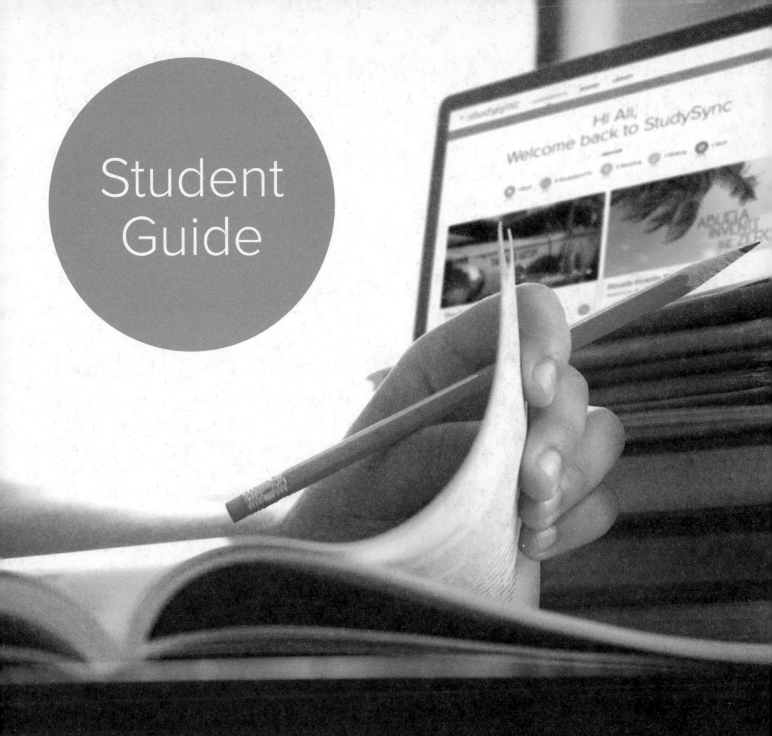

Student Guide

Getting Started

Welcome to the StudySync Reading & Writing Companion! In this book, you will find a collection of readings based on the theme of the unit you are studying. As you work through the readings, you will be asked to answer questions and perform a variety of tasks designed to help you closely analyze and understand each text selection. Read on for an explanation of each

Close Reading and Writing Routine

In each unit, you will read texts that share a common theme, despite their different genres, time periods, and authors. Each reading encourages a closer look through questions and a short writing assignment.

Eleven

FICTION
Sandra Cisneros
1991

Introduction   studysync®

① Introduction

An Introduction to each text provides historical context for your reading as well as information about the author. You will also learn about the genre of the text and the year in which it was written.

Sandra Cisneros (b. 1954) is a renowned Chicana writer whose poems, novels, and short stories explore the complicated struggle of finding one's own identity. Cisneros is best known for her novel *The House on Mango Street* and the collection *Woman Hollering Creek and Other Stories*. "Eleven" is from the latter, the story of a girl named Rachel who experiences growing pains on her eleventh birthday. When her teacher insists that an ugly red sweater belongs to Rachel, the eleven-year-old has exceptional thoughts but can't share them. Even so, it's evident that the protagonist of Sandra Cisneros's short story has insight beyond her years.

② Notes

Many times, while working through the activities after each text, you will be asked to **annotate** or **make annotations** about what you are reading. This means that you should highlight or underline words in the text and use the "Notes" column to make comments or jot down any questions you have. You may also want to note any unfamiliar vocabulary words here.

You will also see sample student annotations to go along with the Skill lesson for that text.

Eleven

"You open your eyes and everything's just like yesterday, only it's today. And you don't feel eleven at all."

What they don't understand about birthdays and what they never tell you is that when you're eleven, you're also ten, and nine, and eight, and seven, and six, and five, and four, and three, and two, and one. And when you wake up on your eleventh birthday you expect to feel eleven, but you don't. You open your eyes and everything's just like yesterday, only it's today. And you don't feel eleven at all. You feel like you're still ten. And you are—underneath the year that makes you eleven.

Like some days you might say something stupid, and that's the part of you that's still ten. Or maybe some days you might need to sit on your mama's lap because you're scared, and that's the part of you that's five. And maybe one day when you're all grown up maybe you will need to cry like if you're three, and that's okay. That's what I tell Mama when she's sad and needs to cry. Maybe she's feeling three.

Because the way you grow old is kind of like an onion or like the rings inside a tree trunk or like my little wooden dolls that fit one inside the other, each year inside the next one. That's how being eleven years old is.

You don't feel eleven. Not right away. It takes a few days, weeks even, sometimes even months before you say Eleven when they ask you. And you don't feel smart eleven, not until you're almost twelve. That's the way it is.

Only today I wish I didn't have only eleven years rattling inside me like pennies in a tin Band-Aid box. Today I wish I was one hundred and two instead of eleven because if I was one hundred and two I'd have known what to say when Mrs. Price put the red sweater on my desk. I would've known how to tell her it wasn't mine instead of just sitting there with that look on my face and nothing coming out of my mouth.

"Whose is this?" Mrs. Price says, and she holds the red sweater up in the air for all the class to see. "Whose? It's been sitting in the coatroom for a month."

Skill: Figurative Language

The narrator uses similes when she compares aging to everyday things. When I picture onions, tree trunks, and wooden dolls, I notice they all have layers. She must mean that when you get older, you keep getting more layers.

Reading & Writing Companion

3 First Read

During your first reading of each selection, you should just try to get a general idea of the content and message of the reading. Don't worry if there are parts you don't understand or words that are unfamiliar to you. You'll have an opportunity later to dive deeper into the text.

4 Think Questions

These questions will ask you to start thinking critically about the text, asking specific questions about its purpose, and making connections to your prior knowledge and reading experiences. To answer these questions, you should go back to the text and draw upon specific evidence to support your responses. You will also begin to explore some of the more challenging vocabulary words in the selection.

5 Skills

Each Skill includes two parts: Checklist and Your Turn. In the Checklist, you will learn the process for analyzing the text. The model student annotations in the text provide examples of how you might make your own notes following the instructions in the Checklist. In the Your Turn, you will use those same instructions to practice the skill.

3 First Read

Read "Eleven." After you read, complete the Think Questions below.

4 THINK QUESTIONS

1. How does Rachel feel about the red sweater that is placed on her desk? Respond with textual evidence from the story as well as ideas that you have inferred from clues in the text.

2. According to Rachel, why does Sylvia say the sweater belongs to Rachel? Support your answer with textual evidence.

3. Write two or three sentences exploring why Mrs. Price responds as she does when Phyllis claims the sweater. Support your answer with textual evidence.

4. Find the word **raggedy** in paragraph 9 of "Eleven." Use context clues in the surrounding sentences, as well as the sentence in which the word appears, to determine the word's meaning. Write your definition here and identify clues that helped you figure out its meaning.

5. Use context clues to determine the meaning of **nonsense** as it is used in paragraph 15 of "Eleven." Write your definition here and identify clues that helped you figure out its meaning. Then check the meaning in a dictionary.

5 Skill: Figurative Language

Use the Checklist to analyze Figurative Language in "Eleven." Refer to the sample student annotations about Figurative Language in the text.

CHECKLIST FOR FIGURATIVE LANGUAGE

To determine the meaning of figures of speech in a text, note the following:

✓ words that mean one thing literally and suggest something else
✓ similes, such as "strong as an ox"
✓ metaphors, such as "her eyes were stars"
✓ personification, such as "the daisies danced in the wind"

In order to interpret the meaning of a figure of speech in context, ask the following questions:

✓ Does any of the descriptive language in the text compare two seemingly unlike things?
✓ Do any descriptions include "like" or "as" that indicate a simile?
✓ Is there a direct comparison that suggests a metaphor?
✓ Is a human quality is being used to describe this animal, object, force of nature or idea that suggests personification?
✓ How does the use of this figure of speech change your understanding of the thing or person being described?

YOUR TURN

1. How does the figurative language in paragraph 18 help readers understand Rachel's reaction to the sweater?

   ○ A. The metaphors in the paragraph help readers understand how uncomfortable Rachel feels in the sweater.
   ○ B. The similes in the paragraph help readers understand how uncomfortable Rachel feels in the sweater.
   ○ C. The metaphors in the paragraph make it clear to readers that Rachel is overreacting about the sweater.
   ○ D. The similes in the paragraph make it clear to readers that Rachel is overreacting about the sweater.

2. How does the figurative language in paragraph 19 help readers visualize Rachel's behavior?

   ○ A. The mention of "little animal noises" tells readers that Rachel is acting more like an animal than a human.
   ○ B. The metaphor of "clown-sweater arms" shows that Rachel is able to see the humorous side in her experience.
   ○ C. The similes about her body shaking "like when you have the hiccups" and her head hurting "like when you drink milk too fast" connect to unpleasant experiences most readers have had.
   ○ D. The statement that "there aren't any more tears left in [her] eyes" suggests that Rachel is starting to calm down.

Eleven

Close Read

Reread "Eleven." As you reread, complete the Skills Focus questions below. Then use your answers and annotations from the questions to help you complete the Write activity.

◎ SKILLS FOCUS

1. Identify examples of figurative language and explain the purpose they achieve in the story.

2. Explain what you can infer about the narrator's feelings about the sweater based on her descriptions, actions, and reactions.

3. The narrator uses figurative language, including similes and metaphors, to describe aging. Identify these in the text. Explain what type of figurative language each one is an example of and what each piece of figurative language means.

4. Explain what the author implies about what the narrator really wants when she says, "today I wish I was one hundred and two."

5. Getting older can be tough. Identify and explain the textual evidence in the story that supports this statement.

✎ WRITE

LITERARY ANALYSIS: How does the author's use of figurative language help readers understand the feelings that the narrator is expressing? Write a response of at least 200 words. Support your writing with evidence from the text.

Lost Island

FICTION

Introduction

Marina wakes up alone, thirsty, and hungry on a deserted island. How did she get here, and why is her head throbbing? As she slowly recalls a large wave smashing into Uncle Merlin's fishing boat, Marina takes her first steps towards survival.

▾ VOCABULARY

damp
wet

capsized
tipped over in the water

intense
very strong

rescuer
someone who saves a person from harm or danger

Close Read & Skills Focus

After you have completed the First Read, you will be asked to go back and read the text more closely and critically. Before you begin your Close Read, you should read through the Skills Focus to get an idea of the concepts you will want to focus on during your second reading. You should work through the Skills Focus by making annotations, highlighting important concepts, and writing notes or questions in the "Notes" column. Depending on instructions from your teacher, you may need to respond online or use a separate piece of paper to start expanding on your thoughts and ideas.

Write

Your study of each selection will end with a writing assignment. For this assignment, you should use your notes, annotations, personal ideas, and answers to both the Think and Skills Focus questions. Be sure to read the prompt carefully and address each part of it in your writing.

English Language Learner

The English Language Learner texts focus on improving language proficiency. You will practice learning strategies and skills in individual and group activities to become better readers, writers, and speakers.

Extended Writing Project and Grammar

This is your opportunity to use genre characteristics and craft to compose meaningful, longer written works exploring the theme of each unit. You will draw information from your readings, research, and own life experiences to complete the assignment.

1 Writing Project

After you have read all of the unit text selections, you will move on to a writing project. Each project will guide you through the process of writing your essay. Student models will provide guidance and help you organize your thoughts. One unit ends with an **Extended Oral Project**, which will give you an opportunity to develop your oral language and communication skills.

2 Writing Process Steps

There are four steps in the writing process: Plan, Draft, Revise, and Edit and Publish. During each step, you will form and shape your writing project, and each lesson's peer review will give you the chance to receive feedback from your peers and teacher.

3 Writing Skills

Each Skill lesson focuses on a specific strategy or technique that you will use during your writing project. Each lesson presents a process for applying the skill to your own work and gives you the opportunity to practice it to improve your writing.

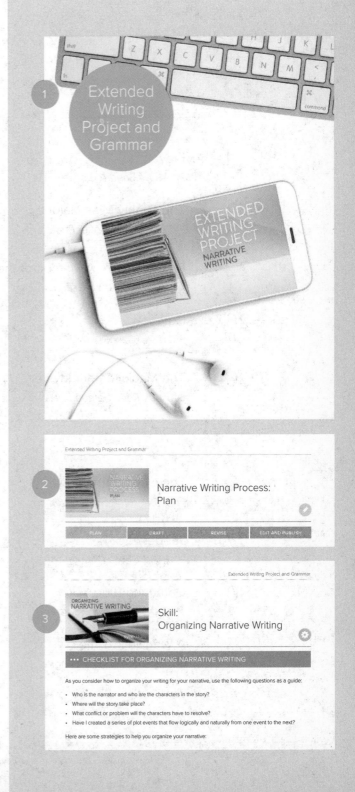

Testing Our Limits

What do we do when life gets hard?

Genre Focus: FICTION

Texts

 Paired Readings

Extended Writing Project and Grammar

Reading & Writing
Companion

Unit 1: Testing Our Limits
What do we do when life gets hard?

AVI

The name Avi (b. 1937) was given to American writer Edward Irving Wortis by his twin sister at an early age. Though he grew up in a highly literate and creative family of writers, artists, and musicians in Brooklyn, writing has never come easily to Avi, who suffers from dysgraphia. Now an author of over seventy-five books—everything from graphic novels to historical fiction and beyond—Avi enjoys showing error-addled drafts of his work to young writers as encouragement.

LEWIS CARROLL

Charles Lutwidge Dodgson, better known by his pen name Lewis Carroll (1832–1898), was a British writer of fiction for children. The author's best-known work, *Alice's Adventures in Wonderland* (1865), showcases his playful language and features "Jabberwocky," which is a nonsense poem about a make-believe creature called the Jabberwock. The poem has been so widely read and loved that some of the made-up words in the poem have entered the English dictionary—like the word "chortle."

SANDRA CISNEROS

A dual citizen of Mexico and the United States, Sandra Cisneros (b. 1954) is a writer of poetry, fiction, and essays. Her books have been translated into over twenty languages, and her novel *The House on Mango Street* is required reading in many schools. Cisneros is interested in how writing may serve as activism. In an *Electric Literature* interview, she argued that "the more you reach into the different things that make you who you are, the more you hold up a mirror to what makes you different from others."

CHRISTOPHER PAUL CURTIS

Christopher Paul Curtis (b. 1953) is an American writer of children's books, many of which are set in his hometown of Flint, Michigan. His award-winning book *Bud, Not Buddy* (1999) is based in part on the author's grandfather, who led the band Herman Curtis and the Dusky Devastators in the 1930s. For Curtis, placing characters against the historical backdrop of the Great Depression is an effective way to highlight the poverty and hunger that millions of people still face every day.

JI-LI JIANG

Ji-li Jiang (b. 1954) is a Chinese American author from Shanghai, who immigrated to Hawaii shortly after the Cultural Revolution. Her memoir *Red Scarf Girl* (1998) details her teenage years in China, where she found her position as Student Council President at odds with her family's political status. Today, Jiang lives in Seattle and promotes cultural exchange between Western countries and China through nonprofit work, and hopes that literature like her memoir can also nurture understanding and acceptance.

MADELEINE L'ENGLE

Madeleine L'Engle (1918–2007), the only child of a writer and a pianist in New York City, wrote her first story at the age of five. She continued writing as she grew up, and after college pursued a career in theater before publishing her first novel about an aspiring pianist. The author waded through an astounding twenty-six rejections before finding a publisher who championed her well-known novel *A Wrinkle in Time* (1962).

LOIS LOWRY

The author of forty-five children's books, Lois Lowry (b. 1937) is an American author who divides her time between Massachusetts and Maine. Her most famous novel, *The Giver* (1993) has three companion novels and takes place in a fictional future in which technology as we know it has been eliminated. Though Lowry has said she always wanted to be a writer and nothing else, she did not imagine writing books for a young audience until she was asked to do so by her publisher in 1977, with the book *A Summer to Die*.

GARY PAULSEN

Gary Paulsen (b. 1939) is a writer of young adult literature from Minnesota. At the age of seven, on a ship bound for the Philippines, Paulsen witnessed a plane crash and looked on as his mother tended to injured passengers. A plane crash figures prominently in his novel *Hatchet* (1987), which follows a young boy's survival after he is stranded in the wilderness. The author wrote a sequel, *Brian's Winter* (1996), after he received as many as two hundred letters a day from readers who wanted to know more of the story.

RENÉ SALDAÑA, JR.

René Saldaña, Jr. is an author and teacher who loosely bases many of his fictional works on his experiences growing up in southern Texas near the border of the United States and Mexico. His stories typically follow pre-teen and teenage characters as they address issues of love, danger, loyalty, and family. As an educator, Saldaña has written and stated the need to "simply validate who kids are" through diversity in literature for young readers.

Eleven

FICTION
Sandra Cisneros
1991

Introduction

S andra Cisneros (b. 1954) is a renowned Chicana writer whose poems, novels, and short stories explore the complicated struggle of finding one's own identity. Cisneros is best known for her novel *The House on Mango Street* and the collection *Woman Hollering Creek and Other Stories*. "Eleven" is from the latter, the story of a girl named Rachel who experiences growing pains on her 11th birthday. When her teacher insists that an ugly red sweater belongs to Rachel, the 11-year-old has exceptional thoughts but can't share them. Even so, it's evident that the protagonist of Sandra Cisneros's short story has insight beyond her years.

"You open your eyes and everything's just like yesterday, only it's today. And you don't feel eleven at all."

Copyright © BookheadEd Learning, LLC

NOTES

1   What they don't understand about birthdays and what they never tell you is that when you're eleven, you're also ten, and nine, and eight, and seven, and six, and five, and four, and three, and two, and one. And when you wake up on your eleventh birthday you expect to feel eleven, but you don't. You open your eyes and everything's just like yesterday, only it's today. And you don't feel eleven at all. You feel like you're still ten. And you are—underneath the year that makes you eleven.

2   Like some days you might say something stupid, and that's the part of you that's still ten. Or maybe some days you might need to sit on your mama's lap because you're scared, and that's the part of you that's five. And maybe one day when you're all grown up maybe you will need to cry like if you're three, and that's okay. That's what I tell Mama when she's sad and needs to cry. Maybe she's feeling three.

3   Because the way you grow old is kind of like an onion or like the rings inside a tree trunk or like my little wooden dolls that fit one inside the other, each year inside the next one. That's how being eleven years old is.

4   You don't feel eleven. Not right away. It takes a few days, weeks even, sometimes even months before you say Eleven when they ask you. And you don't feel smart eleven, not until you're almost twelve. That's the way it is.

5   Only today I wish I didn't have only eleven years rattling inside me like pennies in a tin Band-Aid box. Today I wish I was one hundred and two instead of eleven because if I was one hundred and two I'd have known what to say when Mrs. Price put the red sweater on my desk. I would've known how to tell her it wasn't mine instead of just sitting there with that look on my face and nothing coming out of my mouth.

6   "Whose is this?" Mrs. Price says, and she holds the red sweater up in the air for all the class to see. "Whose? It's been sitting in the coatroom for a month."

7   "Not mine," says everybody, "Not me."

 Skill: Figurative Language

The narrator uses similes when she compares aging to everyday things. When I picture onions, tree trunks, and nested wooden dolls, I notice they all have layers. She must mean that when you get older, you keep getting more layers.

Skill:
Text-Dependent
Responses

Rachel thinks the sweater is old, ugly, and "all stretched out." I don't think she likes it at all.

8   "It has to belong to somebody," Mrs. Price keeps saying, but nobody can remember. It's an ugly sweater with red plastic buttons and a collar and sleeves all stretched out like you could use it for a jump rope. It's maybe a thousand years old and even if it belonged to me I wouldn't say so.

9   Maybe because I'm skinny, maybe because she doesn't like me, that stupid Sylvia Saldivar says, "I think it belongs to Rachel." An ugly sweater like that all **raggedy** and old, but Mrs. Price believes her. Mrs. Price takes the sweater and puts it right on my desk, but when I open my mouth nothing comes out.

10 "That's not, I don't, you're not . . . Not mine." I finally say in a little voice that was maybe me when I was four.

11 "Of course it's yours," Mrs. Price says. "I remember you wearing it once." Because she's older and the teacher, she's right and I'm not.

12 Not mine, not mine, not mine, but Mrs. Price is already turning to page thirty-two, and math problem number four. I don't know why but all of a sudden I'm feeling sick inside, like the part of me that's three wants to come out of my eyes, only I squeeze them shut tight and bite down on my teeth real hard and try to remember today I am eleven, eleven. Mama is making a cake for me for tonight, and when Papa comes home everybody will sing Happy birthday, happy birthday to you.

13 But when the sick feeling goes away and I open my eyes, the red sweater's still sitting there like a big red mountain. I move the red sweater to the corner of my desk with my ruler. I move my pencil and books and eraser as far from it as possible. I even move my chair a little to the right. Not mine, not mine, not mine.

14 In my head I'm thinking how long till lunchtime, how long till I can take the red sweater and throw it over the schoolyard fence, or leave it hanging on a parking meter, or bunch it up into a little ball and toss it in the **alley.** Except when math period ends Mrs. Price says loud and in front of everybody, "Now, Rachel, that's enough," because she sees I've shoved the red sweater to the tippy-tip corner of my desk and it's hanging all over the edge like a waterfall, but I don't care.

15 "Rachel," Mrs. Price says. She says it like she's getting mad. "You put that sweater on right now and no more **nonsense.**"

16 "But it's not—"

17 "Now!" Mrs. Price says.

18 This is when I wish I wasn't eleven because all the years inside of me—ten, nine, eight, seven, six, five, four, three, two, and one—are pushing at the back of my eyes when I put one arm through one sleeve of the sweater that smells

Reading & Writing
Companion

NOTES

like cottage cheese, and then the other arm through the other and stand there with my arms apart like if the sweater hurts me and it does, all itchy and full of **germs** that aren't even mine.

19 That's when everything I've been holding in since this morning, since when Mrs. Price put the sweater on my desk, finally lets go, and all of a sudden I'm crying in front of everybody. I wish I was **invisible** but I'm not. I'm eleven and it's my birthday today and I'm crying like I'm three in front of everybody. I put my head down on the desk and bury my face in my stupid clown-sweater arms. My face all hot and spit coming out of my mouth because I can't stop the little animal noises from coming out of me until there aren't any more tears left in my eyes, and it's just my body shaking like when you have the hiccups, and my whole head hurts like when you drink milk too fast.

20 But the worst part is right before the bell rings for lunch. That stupid Phyllis Lopez, who is even dumber than Sylvia Saldivar, says she remembers the red sweater is hers! I take it off right away and give it to her, only Mrs. Price pretends like everything's okay.

21 Today I'm eleven. There's a cake Mama's making for tonight and when Papa comes home from work we'll eat it. There'll be candles and presents and everybody will sing Happy birthday, happy birthday to you, Rachel, only it's too late.

22 I'm eleven today. I'm eleven, ten, nine, eight, seven, six, five, four, three, two, and one, but I wish I was one hundred and two. I wish I was anything but eleven, because I want today to be far away already, far away like a runaway balloon, like a tiny *o* in the sky, so tiny-tiny you have to close your eyes to see it.

 Skill: Textual Evidence

This is the second time Rachel has called one of her classmates stupid.

Rachel shows just how upset with Mrs. Price she really is by lashing out at her classmates. She is 11, but she is acting like a little kid because she doesn't know how else to act.

From WOMAN HOLLERING CREEK. Copyright ©1991 by Sandra Cisneros. Published by Vintage Books, a division of Random House, Inc., New York and originally in hardcover by Random House, Inc. By permission of Susan Bergholz Literary Services, New York, NY and Lamy, NM. All rights reserved

Please note that excerpts and passages in the StudySync® library and this workbook are intended as touchstones to generate interest in an author's work. The excerpts and passages do not substitute for the reading of entire texts, and StudySync® strongly recommends that students seek out and purchase the whole literary or informational work in order to experience it as the author intended. Links to online resellers are available in our digital library. In addition, complete works may be ordered through an authorized reseller by filling out and returning to StudySync® the order form enclosed in this workbook.

Reading & Writing Companion   3

Skill:
Text-Dependent Responses

Use the Checklist to analyze Text-Dependent Responses in "Eleven." Refer to the sample student annotations about Text-Dependent Responses in the text.

••• CHECKLIST FOR TEXT-DEPENDENT RESPONSES

In order to identify textual evidence to support an analysis of a text, consider the following:

✓ details from the text to make an inference or draw a conclusion. Inferences are logical deductions from information in a text that is not directly, or explicitly, stated by the author

- read carefully and consider why an author gives particular details and information
- think about what you already know and use your own knowledge and experiences to help you figure out what the author does not state directly
- cite textual evidence, or the specific words, phrases, sentences, or paragraphs that led you to make an inference

✓ details that you can use to support your ideas and opinions about a text

✓ explicit evidence of a character's feelings or motivations, or the reasons behind an historical event in a nonfiction text

- explicit evidence is stated directly in the text and must be cited accurately to support a text-dependent answer or analysis

To cite textual evidence to support an analysis, consider the following questions:

✓ What types of textual evidence can I use to support an analysis of a text?

✓ What explicit evidence can I use to support my analysis?

✓ If I infer things in the text that the author does not state directly, what evidence from the text, along with my own experiences and knowledge, can I use to support my analysis?

Skill:
Text-Dependent Responses

Read the second Think question from the First Read lesson for "Eleven." Then, using the Checklist on the previous page, complete the chart by deciding whether the evidence from the text can be used to form a response.

⟳ YOUR TURN

Evidence Options	
A	"Maybe because I'm skinny. . ."
B	"That's not, I don't, you're not . . . Not mine."
C	"Of course it's yours," Mrs. Price says. "I remember you wearing it once."
D	"Maybe because she doesn't like me . . ."

Would Support a Response	Would Not Support a Response

First Read

Read "Eleven." After you read, complete the Think Questions below.

☁ THINK QUESTIONS

1. How does Rachel feel about the red sweater that is placed on her desk? Respond with textual evidence from the story as well as ideas that you have inferred from clues in the text.

2. According to Rachel, why does Sylvia say the sweater belongs to Rachel? Support your answer with textual evidence.

3. Write two or three sentences exploring why Mrs. Price responds as she does when Phyllis claims the sweater. Support your answer with textual evidence.

4. Find the word **raggedy** in paragraph 9 of "Eleven." Use context clues in the surrounding sentences, as well as the sentence in which the word appears, to determine the word's meaning. Write your definition here and identify clues that helped you figure out its meaning.

5. Use context clues to determine the meaning of **nonsense** as it is used in paragraph 15 of "Eleven." Write your definition here and identify clues that helped you figure out its meaning. Then check the meaning in a dictionary.

Please note that excerpts and passages in the StudySync® library and this workbook are intended as touchstones to generate interest in an author's work. The excerpts and passages do not substitute for the reading of entire texts, and StudySync® strongly recommends that students seek out and purchase the whole literary or informational work in order to experience it as the author intended. Links to online resellers are available in our digital library. In addition, complete works may be ordered through an authorized reseller by filling out and returning to StudySync® the order form enclosed in this workbook.

Skill:
Textual Evidence

Use the Checklist to analyze Textual Evidence in "Eleven." Refer to the sample student annotations about Textual Evidence in the text.

••• CHECKLIST FOR TEXTUAL EVIDENCE

To support an analysis by citing textual evidence that is explicitly, or clearly, stated in the text, do the following:

- ✓ read the text closely and critically

- ✓ identify what the text says explicitly

- ✓ find the most relevant textual evidence that supports your analysis and ideas

- ✓ consider why an author explicitly states specific details and information

- ✓ cite the specific words, phrases, sentences, or paragraphs from the text that support your analysis and ideas

In order to interpret implicit meanings in a text by making inferences, do the following:

- ✓ combine information directly stated in the text with your own knowledge, experiences, and observations

- ✓ cite the specific words, phrases, sentences, or paragraphs from the text that led to and support this inference.

In order to cite textual evidence to support an analysis of what the text says explicitly as well as inferences drawn from the text, consider the following questions:

- ✓ Have I read the text closely and critically?

- ✓ What inferences am I making about the text? What textual evidence am I using to support these inferences?

- ✓ Am I quoting the evidence from the text correctly?

- ✓ Does my textual evidence logically relate to my analysis and ideas?

Please note that excerpts and passages in the StudySync® library and this workbook are intended as touchstones to generate interest in an author's work. The excerpts and passages do not substitute for the reading of entire texts, and StudySync® strongly recommends that students seek out and purchase the whole literary or informational work in order to experience it as the author intended. Links to online resellers are available in our digital library. In addition, complete works may be ordered through an authorized reseller by filling out and returning to StudySync® the order form enclosed in this workbook.

Reading & Writing Companion

7

Skill:
Textual Evidence

Read the following excerpts from the story. Then, match the evidence found explicitly in the text and the inference drawn from the text for each excerpt. The first one is done for you.

⟳ YOUR TURN

	Evidence Options
A	The narrator dislikes the old sweater and wants to distance herself from it.
B	Because Mrs. Price is older and the teacher, her opinion about the sweater is correct.
C	Rachel is saying that Mrs. Price makes her feel powerless.
D	The narrator thinks the sweater is old, and she dislikes it.

Text	Evidence found explicitly in the text	Inference drawn from the text
Today I wish I was one hundred and two instead of eleven because if I was one hundred and two I'd have known what to say when Mrs. Price put the red sweater on my desk.	The narrator wishes she were 102 years old.	The narrator wishes she were older so she would know how to deal with difficult situations.
It's maybe a thousand years old and even if it belonged to me I wouldn't say so.		
"Of course it's yours," Mrs. Price says. "I remember you wearing it once." Because she's older and the teacher, she's right and I'm not.		

Reading & Writing Companion

Skill:
Figurative Language

Use the Checklist to analyze Figurative Language in "Eleven." Refer to the sample student annotations about Figurative Language in the text.

••• CHECKLIST FOR FIGURATIVE LANGUAGE

To determine the meaning of figures of speech in a text, note the following:

- ✓ words that mean one thing literally and suggest something else
- ✓ similes, such as "strong as an ox"
- ✓ metaphors, such as "her eyes were stars"
- ✓ personification, such as "the daisies danced in the wind"

In order to interpret the meaning of a figure of speech in context, ask the following questions:

- ✓ Does any of the descriptive language in the text compare two seemingly unlike things?
- ✓ Do any descriptions include "like" or "as" that indicate a simile?
- ✓ Is there a direct comparison that suggests a metaphor?
- ✓ Is a human quality is being used to describe this animal, object, force of nature or idea that suggests personification?
- ✓ How does the use of this figure of speech change your understanding of the thing or person being described?

In order to analyze the impact of figurative language on the meaning of a text, use the following questions as a guide:

- ✓ Where does figurative language appear in the text? What does it mean?
- ✓ Why does the author use figurative language rather than literal language?

Please note that excerpts and passages in the StudySync® library and this workbook are intended as touchstones to generate interest in an author's work. The excerpts and passages do not substitute for the reading of entire texts, and StudySync® strongly recommends that students seek out and purchase the whole literary or informational work in order to experience it as the author intended. Links to online resellers are available in our digital library. In addition, complete works may be ordered through an authorized reseller by filling out and returning to StudySync® the order form enclosed in this workbook.

Reading & Writing Companion   9

Skill:
Figurative Language

Reread paragraphs 14 and 19 of "Eleven." Then, using the Checklist on the previous page, answer the multiple-choice questions below.

⟳ YOUR TURN

1. How does the figurative language in paragraph 14 help readers understand Rachel's reaction to the sweater?

   ○ A. The metaphors in the paragraph help readers understand how Rachel feels about the sweater.

   ○ B. The simile in the paragraph helps readers understand how Rachel feels about the sweater.

   ○ C. The metaphors in the paragraph make it clear to readers that Rachel is overreacting about the sweater.

   ○ D. The simile in the paragraph makes it clear to readers that Rachel is overreacting about the sweater.

2. How does the figurative language in paragraph 19 help readers visualize Rachel's behavior?

   ○ A. The mention of "little animal noises" tells readers that Rachel is acting more like an animal than a human.

   ○ B. The metaphor of "clown-sweater arms" shows that Rachel is able to see the humorous side in her experience.

   ○ C. The similes about her body shaking "like when you have the hiccups" and her head hurting "like when you drink milk too fast" connect to unpleasant experiences most readers have had.

   ○ D. The statement that "there aren't any more tears left in [her] eyes" suggests that Rachel is starting to calm down.

Close Read

Reread "Eleven." As you reread, complete the Skills Focus questions below. Then use your answers and annotations from the questions to help you complete the Write activity.

◎ SKILLS FOCUS

1. Identify examples of figurative language and explain the purpose they achieve in the story.

2. Explain what you can infer about the narrator's feelings about the sweater based on her descriptions, actions, and reactions.

3. The narrator uses figurative language, including similes and metaphors, to describe aging. Identify these in the text. Explain what type of figurative language each one is an example of and what each piece of figurative language means.

4. Explain what the author implies about what the narrator really wants when she says, "today I wish I was one hundred and two."

5. Getting older can be tough. Identify and explain the textual evidence in the story that supports this statement.

✏ WRITE

LITERARY ANALYSIS: How does the author's use of figurative language help readers understand the feelings that the narrator is expressing? Support your writing with evidence from the text.

Please note that excerpts and passages in the StudySync® library and this workbook are intended as touchstones to generate interest in an author's work. The excerpts and passages do not substitute for the reading of entire texts, and StudySync® strongly recommends that students seek out and purchase the whole literary or informational work in order to experience it as the author intended. Links to online resellers are available in our digital library. In addition, complete works may be ordered through an authorized reseller by filling out and returning to StudySync® the order form enclosed in this workbook.

Reading & Writing Companion   11

The Mighty Miss Malone

FICTION
Christopher Paul Curtis
2012

Introduction

The Mighty Miss Malone is author Christopher Paul Curtis's follow-up to 2000's Newbery award-winning *Bud, Not Buddy*—both stories of young African Americans set in Great Depression-era Flint, Michigan. This time, 12-year-old Deza Malone—new in Flint from Gary, Indiana, where she was at the top of her class—is the narrator. When her father doesn't return from a trip to find work, Deza, her brother Jimmie, and her mother go looking for him, journeying across the land by hopping aboard a boxcar. For a time, the Malones make their home outside of Flint, Michigan, in a "Hooverville," a ragtag encampment of hoboes and wayfarers. When Deza begins again at a new school, her teachers, unlike her beloved former teacher Mrs. Needham, treat her unfairly because of her race. As this excerpt begins, Deza

"You must be a genius to get a C plus!"

NOTES

from Chapter Twenty-Two: Learning How to Settle in Flint

1   I'd been having such a good time being Little Stew and trying to fill in all the missing words from the *Reader's Digest* that time had completely run off and forgot all about me!

2   "But, Mother, Miss Stew needs me to—"

3   "You aren't suggesting you stay here and help Stew instead of going to school, are you?" When she said it like that, it did seem silly.

. . .

4   On the outside, schools in Flint seemed a lot like schools in Gary, but they weren't. Instead of having one teacher all day, in Flint we went from classroom to classroom and teacher to teacher for each subject. The teachers were different too. First, all of them were white, and second, they weren't anywhere as nice as the teachers in Gary. But one of Mrs. Needham's lessons stuck: I was learning how to toughen up.

5   I got my usual As on the tests in mathematics, geography, civics and history.

6   After my first mathematics test, when class was dismissed, Mrs. Scott called me to her desk.

7   "Deza, have you always done so well in math? You're the only student who got a perfect score."

8   I sounded very **humble,** but the truth's the truth. "Yes, ma'am. Mathematics is one of my favorite subjects."

9   It was great to be back in school!

10   "Could I ask you a favor?"

11   Maybe she wanted me to help some of my classmates. Even though they were white, some of them were the spittin' image of Dolly Peaches and Benny Cobb.

12   She slid a paper toward me. It had five unsolved story problems on it.

13   "Could you sit right there, right now, and solve these for me?"

14   Maybe Mrs. Scott was seeing if I was ready for harder work. I finished in no time.

15   She looked them over. "Hmm, perfect again, but next time you *must* make sure to show all your work. You're dismissed."

16   I was surprised that was all she said.

17   In English class I *really* showed how much I'd toughened up.

18   Flint teachers don't have the imaginations that Gary teachers do, so instead of giving grades back so everyone knows what you got, they walk around the class and hand your test or paper back to you. Upside down.

19   Mr. Smith was passing out our first essay. I'd followed all of Mrs. Needham's advice. I'd written it at the Flint Public Library and was very careful not to use the dictionary or the thesaurus too much. And I didn't **digress** at all.

20   I made sure my posture was good, crossed my ankles and folded my hands on the desk when he got close to me.

21   He handed me my paper and smiled. "Very good job."

22   My heart flew! "Thank you, sir."

23   I turned my paper over.

24   He'd written, "Good for you!" and put a giant C+ with three exclamation points.

25   I turned the paper back over. Maybe I saw it wrong.

26   I looked again but it was the same.

27   One sign that I had toughened up was that instead of crying I thought of a little joke that Jimmie said he did whenever he didn't like his grade.

28   "I turn the paper over, then, the same way people bang on a machine it if ain't acting right, I smack my hand on the paper. Maybe if I bang it hard enough my grade will jump up a mark!"

29   It was nonsense, but I slapped my hand on Mr. Smith's essay.

30   I turned the paper back over and smiled.

Skill:
Character

Deza's reaction to her grade is to follow her brother's advice. When Deza turns the paper over, I notice she doesn't start crying or anything. She smiles. This reaction shows me that Deza knows her essay is good. She's changed—before she would have cried, but now she's strong.

31   I'd have to tell Jimmie that it still wasn't working.

32   Mrs. Needham would've been proud. Instead of bawling, I looked at Mr. Smith's back and said to myself, "OK, buster, I'm going to make sure my next essay is the best thing I've ever written. You won't have any choice but to give me my A plus."

33   When me and Loretta were walking back to camp I asked, "What grade did you get on your essay?"

34   "I don't know, the same old D. What'd you get?"

35   "C plus."

36   She stopped walking. "Uh-oh, no, you didn't!"

37   I showed her my grade.

38   "Ooh, girl, you must be *real* smart."

39   "For getting a C plus?"

40   "All these teachers up here at Whittier's prejudice. Katherine Williams was the smartest colored girl in the school and all she use to get was a C. You must be a genius to get a C plus!"

41   She laughed. "I'm gonna see if I can sit next to you when we take our next exam!"

· · ·

42   Early every morning, Mother and I would leave the camp and walk for half a hour to downtown Flint. Jimmie would go his own way.

43   After school I'd go to the library and read until Mother picked me up. We didn't have a official address so I couldn't check out any books, but I still got to read.

44   It wasn't long before we stopped looking fresh and had **seniority** in camp. Stew said I had a **bubbly** personality so she had me help the new children get used to living here. Some of them didn't have any idea what to do, mostly the boys.

45   I pretended they were my students and was very patient.

46   Two little boys from Flint came in one day all by themselves. One of them reminded me of myself. He seemed scareder than his friend so I took him under my wing.

47   He was very nervous and shy, but you could see how sweet he was too.

Skill:
Character

Instead of complaining about her grade, Deza feels inspired to prove her teacher wrong. Instead of feeling sorry for herself, Deza is determined to impress her teacher and get a better grade.

Please note that excerpts and passages in the StudySync® library and this workbook are intended as touchstones to generate interest in an author's work. The excerpts and passages do not substitute for the reading of entire texts, and StudySync® strongly recommends that students seek out and purchase the whole literary or informational work in order to experience it as the author intended. Links to online resellers are available in our digital library. In addition, complete works may be ordered through an authorized reseller by filling out and returning to StudySync® the order form enclosed in this workbook.

Reading & Writing Companion   **15**

48 His first evening in the camp, I didn't want him and his friend to think they were going to get a free ride so I had them help me with the dishes. I took the little boy and showed him the creek where we clean the camp's pots and dishes. We sat on a big rock and I washed and had him dry.

49 He said, "Are you leaving on the train tomorrow?"

50 "Uh-uh." I'd been lying so much about how we weren't alone that without thinking, I said, "My father's going out on it, he might leave for a day or two for work."

51 "Where do you go to school?"

52 "Well, Mother says I might have to keep going here in Flint at Whittier."

53 The sad-eyed little boy said, "I'm hopping the freight to go west, me and Bugs are gonna pick fruit."

54 "I wish you two well."

55 I'd hand him the dish after I'd washed it and when my hand touched his he'd start blinking a lot and would get twitchity and **fumble** the cloth when he tried to dry the dish.

56 After a while I started touching his hand just to make him squirm. And squirm he did!

57 He counted softly, "One, two, three . . . ," then blurted out, "I'MNOTAFRAIDOFGIRLS!"

58 I laughed. "You aren't?"

59 "Uh-uh. I even kissed some in the home."

60 "Really?"

61 "Yup, I got three kisses."

62 He held up four fingers.

63 I looked up at the moon. It was huge and yellow and yolky. "Isn't the moon lovely?"

64 I looked back. The little boy had closed his eyes, puckered his lips and leaned in toward me!

65 I started to slug him, just a arm punch. But looking at how sad he was made my heart melt.

66 He was all alone except for a person named Bugs.

67   What else could I do?

68   I kissed his forehead three times and said, "Kisses . . . kisses . . . kisses make you stronger."

69   He blinked six or seven times and when his eyes came open he looked lost and befumbled.

70   I put his hand in mine.

71   The harmonica man started playing "Shenandoah."

72   "Do you know that song?"

73   His head was wobbling back and forth and I wasn't sure if he was saying no or getting ready to swoon.

74   I said, "It's about a Indian princess who hasn't seen her husband for seven years."

75   I sang a little.

76   He said, "You sing beautiful."

77   Wow! He *was* befumbled!

78   "You should hear my brother, now that's a real singer."

79   I helped him up and we carried the dishes back to the camp.

80   As bad as things were for me, they were much worse for him. I still had my family, and like Mother always says, without a family you're nothing but dust on the wind.

81   I hoped he'd find kindness somewhere, but even with my exploding imagination, I couldn't figure out where that would be.

Excerpted from *The Mighty Miss Malone* by Christopher Paul Curtis, published by Wendy Lamb Books.

Please note that excerpts and passages in the StudySync® library and this workbook are intended as touchstones to generate interest in an author's work. The excerpts and passages do not substitute for the reading of entire texts, and StudySync® strongly recommends that students seek out and purchase the whole literary or informational work in order to experience it as the author intended. Links to online resellers are available in our digital library. In addition, complete works may be ordered through an authorized reseller by filling out and returning to StudySync® the order form enclosed in this workbook.

Reading & Writing
Companion   17

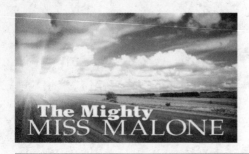

First Read

Read *The Mighty Miss Malone*. After you read, complete the Think Questions below.

☁ THINK QUESTIONS

1. What are the differences between Deza's old school in Gary, Indiana, and her new school in Flint, Michigan? Cite textual evidence to support your answer.

2. Write two or three sentences describing how Loretta reacts when she finds out what grade Deza received on her essay. Support your answer with evidence from the text.

3. What does Deza's attitude toward the little boy she meets in the camp reveal about her character? Cite textual evidence from the selection to support your answer.

4. Find the word **seniority** in paragraph 44 of "The Mighty Miss Malone." Use context clues in the surrounding sentences, as well as the sentence in which the word appears, to determine the word's meaning. Write your definition here and identify clues that helped you figure out the meaning.

5. Use context clues to determine the meaning of **fumble** as it is used in paragraph 55 of "The Mighty Miss Malone." Write your definition here and identify clues that helped you figure out the meaning. Then check the meaning in the dictionary.

Skill:
Character

Use the Checklist to analyze Character in *The Mighty Miss Malone*. Refer to the sample student annotations about Character in the text.

••• CHECKLIST FOR CHARACTER

In order to determine how the characters respond or change as the plot moves toward a resolution, note the following:

✓ the characters in the story, including the protagonist and antagonist

✓ key events or series of episodes in the plot, especially events that cause characters to react, respond, or change in some way

✓ characters' responses as the plot reaches a climax, and moves toward a resolution of the problem facing the protagonist

✓ the resolution of the conflict in the plot and the ways that it affects each character

To describe how a particular story's or drama's plot unfolds in a series of episodes as well as how the characters respond or change as the plot moves toward a resolution, consider the following questions:

✓ How do the characters' responses change or develop from the beginning to the end of the story?

✓ Do the characters in the story change? Which event or events in the story cause a character to change?

✓ Is there an event in the story that provokes, or causes, a character to make a decision?

✓ Do the characters' problems reach a resolution? How?

✓ How does the resolution affect the characters?

Please note that excerpts and passages in the StudySync® library and this workbook are intended as touchstones to generate interest in an author's work. The excerpts and passages do not substitute for the reading of entire texts, and StudySync® strongly recommends that students seek out and purchase the whole literary or informational work in order to experience it as the author intended. Links to online resellers are available in our digital library. In addition, complete works may be ordered through an authorized reseller by filling out and returning to StudySync® the order form enclosed in this workbook.

Reading & Writing
Companion

19

Skill: Character

Reread paragraphs 6–16 from the text. Then, using the Checklist on the previous page, answer the multiple-choice questions below.

↻ YOUR TURN

1. Based on Mrs. Scott's actions in paragraphs 12 and 13, the reader can conclude that —

   ○ A. Mrs. Scott wanted Deza to solve more math problems for extra credit.
   ○ B. Mrs. Scott suspects that Deza may have cheated on her math test.
   ○ C. Deza did not finish the test.
   ○ D. Mrs. Scott wanted to see if Deza was good enough to be a tutor.

2. This question has two parts. First, answer Part A. Then, answer Part B.

   Part A: Deza's reaction to Mrs. Scott's request reveals that Deza —

   ○ A. is anxious to help other students succeed in math.
   ○ B. is aware that Mrs. Scott thinks she might have cheated on her test.
   ○ C. is not aware that Mrs. Scott thinks she might have cheated on her test.
   ○ D. is aware that Mrs. Scott is prejudiced against African American students.

   Part B: Which paragraph best shows evidence for the answer to Part A?

   ○ A. 8
   ○ B. 9
   ○ C. 15
   ○ D. 16

Close Read

Reread *The Mighty Miss Malone*. As you reread, complete the Skills Focus questions below. Then use your answers and annotations from the questions to help you complete the Write activity.

◎ SKILLS FOCUS

1. Recall Deza's initial thoughts about what her Flint teachers say and do. Explain what these thoughts reveal about Deza's character.

2. Focus on Deza's words and actions as she interacts with the little boys who come to the camp. Identify what these indicate about her character.

3. Analyze how Deza's responses to change develop the plot by identifying evidence that shows how her relationship with the camp and Flint changes over time.

4. When life gets hard for Deza, what does she do? Identify evidence of her reactions to challenges and explain whether there are any differences between her thoughts and actions.

✏ WRITE

NARRATIVE: Describe how Deza's responses to the C+ she received on her essay show how her character has changed. Then imagine how she will approach the next assignment she receives from Mr. Smith. Use the information you learned about both characters to write a short scene that describes this event.

Please note that excerpts and passages in the StudySync® library and this workbook are intended as touchstones to generate interest in an author's work. The excerpts and passages do not substitute for the reading of entire texts, and StudySync® strongly recommends that students seek out and purchase the whole literary or informational work in order to experience it as the author intended. Links to online resellers are available in our digital library. In addition, complete works may be ordered through an authorized reseller by filling out and returning to StudySync® the order form enclosed in this workbook.

Reading & Writing Companion   21

Red Scarf Girl: A Memoir of the Cultural Revolution

INFORMATIONAL TEXT

Ji-li Jiang

1997

Introduction

studysync tv

*R*ed Scarf Girl: A Memoir of the Cultural Revolution is an autobiography about the teenage life of Ji-li Jiang, who lived with her family in Shanghai during the 1960s when Communist Party leader Mao Zedong effectively declared war against capitalist and anti-establishment forces throughout China. As Zedong launched a series of purges aimed at purifying the Communist party, Ji-li and her family were dedicated Communists; she was initially embarrassed by her family's "landlord" background when the Cultural Revolution began in 1966. However, her feelings began to change when the government started attacking her family. In this excerpt, she has been pulled out of class and is being interrogated by people from her father's theater.

"I saw Dad looking at me hopelessly, tears on his face."

NOTES

1   "Sit down, sit down. Don't be afraid." Chairman Jin pointed to the empty chair. "These comrades from your father's work unit are just here to have a study session with you. It's nothing to worry about."

2   I sat down dumbly.

3   I had thought about their coming to my home but never imagined this. They were going to **expose** my family in front of my teachers and classmates. I would have no pride left. I would never be an educable child again.

4   Thin-Face sat opposite me, with a woman I had never seen before. Teacher Zhang was there too, his eyes encouraging me.

5   Thin-Face came straight to the point. "Your father's problems are very serious." His cold eyes nailed me to my seat. "You may have read the article in the *Workers' Revolt* that exposed your family's filthy past." I slumped down in my chair without taking my eyes off his face. "In addition to coming from a landlord family, your father committed some serious mistakes during the Antirightist Movement[1] several years ago, but he still obstinately refuses to confess." His cold manner became a little more animated. "Of course we won't tolerate this. We have decided to make an example of him. We are going to have a struggle meeting of the entire theater system to criticize him and force him to confess." He suddenly pounded the table with his fist. The cups on the table rattled.

6   I tore my eyes away from him and stared at a cup instead.

7   "As I told you before, you are your own person. If you want to make a clean break with your black family, then you can be an educable child and we will welcome you to our **revolutionary** ranks." He gave Chairman Jin a look, and Chairman Jin chimed in, "That's right, we welcome you."

8   "Jiang Ji-li has always done well at school. In addition to doing very well in her studies, she participates in educational reform," Teacher Zhang added.

---

1. **Antirightist Movement** a campaign, from roughly 1957 to 1959, to purge people in the Communist Party with alleged capitalist or anti-establishment sympathies

9   "That's very good. We knew that you had more sense than to follow your father," Thin-Face said with a brief, frozen smile. "Now you can show your revolutionary determination." He paused. "We want you to **testify** against your father at the struggle meeting."

10 I closed my eyes. I saw Dad standing on a stage, his head bowed, his name written in large black letters, and then crossed out in red ink, on a sign hanging from his neck. I saw myself standing in the middle of the stage, facing thousands of people, condemning Dad for his crimes, raising my fist to lead the chant, "Down with Jiang Xi-reng." I saw Dad looking at me hopelessly, tears on his face.

11 "I...I..." I looked at Teacher Zhang for help. He looked away.

12 The Woman from the theater spoke. "It's really not such a hard thing to do. The key is your class stance. The daughter of our former Party Secretary resolved to make a clean break with her mother. When she went onstage to condemn her mother, she actually slapped her face. Of course, we don't mean that you have to slap your father's face. The point is that as long as you have the correct class stance, it will be easy to testify." Her voice grated on my ears.

13 "There is something you can do to prove you are truly Chairman Mao's child." Thin-Face spoke again. "I am sure you can tell us some things your father said and did that show his landlord and rightist mentality." I stared at the table, but I could feel his eyes boring into me. "What can you tell us?"

14 "But I don't know anything," I whispered." I don't know—"

15 "I am sure you can remember something if you think about it," Thin-Face said. "A man like him could not hide his true beliefs from a child as smart as you. He must have made comments **critical** of Chairman Mao and the Cultural Revolution. I am sure you are loyal to Chairman Mao and the Communist Party[2]. Tell us!"

16 "But my father never said anything against Chairman Mao," I protested weakly. "I would tell you if he did." My voice grew stronger with conviction. "He never said anything against the Party."

2. **Communist Party** the ruling party of the People's Republic of China, established in 1949 and led by Chairman Mao Zedong

17 "Now, you have to choose between two roads." Thin-Face looked straight into my eyes. "You can break with your family and follow Chairman Mao, or you can follow your father and become an enemy of the people." His voice grew more **severe.** "In that case we would have many more study sessions, with your brother and sister too, and the Red Guard Committee[3] and the school leaders. Think about it. We will come back to talk to you again."

18 Thin-Face and the woman left, saying they would be back to get my statement. Without knowing how I got there, I found myself in a narrow passageway between the school building and the school-yard wall. The gray concrete walls closed around me and a slow drizzle dampened my cheeks. I could not go back to the classroom, and I could not go home. I felt like a small animal that had fallen into a trap, alone and helpless, and sure that the hunter was coming.

Excerpted from *Red Scarf Girl* by Ji-li Jiang, published by HarperCollins Publishers

✏ WRITE

PERSONAL RESPONSE: Jiang is facing a challenging decision—between defending her father and protecting herself. Think about a time you had to make a difficult decision. Explain the decision you had to make, why you had to make it, and who, if anyone, helped you. Does your experience help you empathize with Jiang? Use evidence from the text to support your response.

3. **Red Guard Committee** a student paramilitary organization that organized on behalf of Chairman Mao and the Communist Party, using violence as a means of coercion

Hatchet

FICTION
Gary Paulsen
1987

Introduction

*H*atchet is the first in a series of five novels by Gary Paulsen (b. 1939), who won a Newbery Honor in 1988 for this gripping tale of survival. The hero of *Hatchet* and its follow-ups is young Brian Robeson, who must rely on his wits and instincts alone to stay alive in the Canadian wilderness. Preceding this excerpt from Chapter 5, 13-year-old Brian is left stranded on his own after his pilot has a heart attack and their plane crashes in a lake. The excerpt describes the day

"Nothing.
It kept coming back to that.
He had nothing."

from Chapter 5

1   They would look for him, look for the plane. His father and mother would be frantic. They would tear the world apart to find him. Brian had seen searches on the news, seen movies about lost planes. When a plane went down they mounted **extensive** searches and almost always they found the plane within a day or two. Pilots all filed flight plans—a detailed plan for where and when they were going to fly, with all the courses explained. They would come, they would look for him. The searchers would get government planes and cover both sides of the flight plan filed by the pilot and search until they found him.

2   Maybe even today. They might come today. This was the second day after the crash. No. Brian frowned. Was it the first day or the second day? They had gone down in the afternoon and he had spent the whole night out cold. So this was the first real day. But they could still come today. They would have started the search immediately when Brian's plane did not arrive.

3   Yeah, they would probably come today.

4   Probably come in here with **amphibious** planes, small bushplanes with floats that could land right here on the lake and pick him up and take him home.

5   Which home? The father home or the mother home. He stopped the thinking. It didn't matter. Either on to his dad or back to his mother. Either way he would probably be home by late night or early morning, home where he could sit down and eat a large, cheesy, juicy burger with tomatoes and double fries with ketchup and a thick chocolate shake.

6   And there came hunger.

7   Brian rubbed his stomach. The hunger had been there but something else—fear, pain—had held it down. Now, with the thought of the burger, the emptiness roared at him. He could not believe the hunger, had never felt it this way. The lake water had filled his stomach but left it hungry, and now it demanded food, screamed for food.

8   And there was, he thought, absolutely nothing to eat.

Skill:
Setting

It's obvious that Brian is anxious to be rescued. He's alone and afraid in the wilderness. He's trying to calm himself down by guessing when his rescuers will come, but he has no idea if they ever will.

Copyright © BookheadEd Learning, LLC

NOTES

9   Nothing.

10   What did they do in the movies when they got stranded like this? Oh, yes, the hero usually found some kind of plant that he knew was good to eat and that took care of it. Just ate the plant until he was full or used some kind of cute trap to catch an animal and cook it over a slick little fire and pretty soon he had a full eight-course meal.

11   The trouble, Brian thought, looking around, was that all he could see was grass and brush. There was nothing **obvious** to eat and aside from about a million birds and the beaver he hadn't seen animals to trap and cook, and even if he got one somehow he didn't have any matches so he couldn't have a fire. . .

12   Nothing.

13   It kept coming back to that. He had nothing.

14   Well, almost nothing. As a matter of fact, he thought, I don't know what I've got or haven't got. Maybe I should try and figure out just how I stand. It will give me something to do—keep me from thinking of food. Until they come to find me.

15   Brian had once had an English teacher, a guy named Perpich, who was always talking about being positive, thinking positive, staying on top of things. That's how Perpich had put it—stay positive and stay on top of things. Brian thought of him now—wondered how to stay positive and stay on top of this. All Perpich would say is that I have to get **motivated.** He was always telling kids to get motivated.

16   Brian changed position so he was sitting on his knees. He reached into his pockets and took out everything he had and laid it on the grass in front of him.

17   It was pitiful enough. A quarter, three dimes, a nickel, and two pennies. A fingernail clipper. A billfold with a twenty dollar bill—"In case you get stranded at the airport in some small town and have to buy food," his mother had said—and some odd pieces of paper.

18   And on his belt, somehow still there, the hatchet his mother had given him. He had forgotten it and now reached around and took it out and put it in the grass. There was a touch of rust already forming on the cutting edge of the blade and he rubbed it off with his thumb.

19   That was it.

20   He frowned. No, wait—if he was going to play the game, might as well play it right. Perpich would tell him to quit messing around. Get motivated. Look at *all* of it, Robeson.

21 He had on a pair of good tennis shoes, now almost dry. And socks. And jeans and underwear and a thin leather belt and a T-shirt with a windbreaker so torn it hung on him in tatters.

22 And a watch. He had a digital watch still on his wrist but it was broken from the crash—the little screen blank—and he took it off and almost threw it away but stopped the hand motion and lay the watch on the grass with the rest of it.

23 There. That was it.

24 No, wait. One other thing. Those were all the things he had, but he also had himself. Perpich used to drum that into them—"You are your most valuable **asset.** Don't forget that. *You* are the best thing you have."

25 Brian looked around again. I wish you were here, Perpich. I'm hungry and I'd trade everything I have for a hamburger.

Excerpted from *Hatchet* by Gary Paulsen, published by Simon & Schuster.

Please note that excerpts and passages in the StudySync® library and this workbook are intended as touchstones to generate interest in an author's work. The excerpts and passages do not substitute for the reading of entire texts, and StudySync® strongly recommends that students seek out and purchase the whole literary or informational work in order to experience it as the author intended. Links to online resellers are available in our digital library. In addition, complete works may be ordered through an authorized reseller by filling out and returning to StudySync® the order form enclosed in this workbook.

Reading & Writing Companion   29

First Read

Read *Hatchet*. After you read, complete the Think Questions below.

☁ **THINK QUESTIONS**

1. What happens to Brian? What problem does he have? Cite textual evidence from the selection to support your answer.

2. What is Brian's family situation? What makes you think so? State details from the text or ideas you have inferred from clues in the text.

3. Figurative language is language used for descriptive effect, often to illustrate or imply ideas indirectly. A type of figurative language is **personification**, in which an animal, object, force of nature, or an idea is given human form or qualities. Can you identify an example of personification from *Hatchet* that illustrates one of the problems Brian is facing? Cite textual evidence from the selection to support your answer.

4. Find the word **obvious** as used in paragraph 11 in *Hatchet*. Use context clues in the surrounding sentences, as well as the sentence in which the word appears, to determine the word's meaning. Write your definition here and identify clues that helped you figure out its meaning.

5. Use context clues to determine the meaning of **asset** as it is used in paragraph 24 of the excerpt. Write your definition here and identify clues that helped you figure out its meaning. Then check the meaning in a dictionary.

Skill:
Setting

Use the Checklist to analyze Setting in *Hatchet*. Refer to the sample student annotations about Setting in the text.

••• CHECKLIST FOR SETTING

In order to identify how a particular story's or drama's plot unfolds in a series of episodes, note the following:

- ✓ key elements in the plot
- ✓ the setting(s) in the story
- ✓ how the plot unfolds in a series of episodes
- ✓ how the setting shapes the plot

To describe how a particular story's or drama's plot unfolds in a series of episodes, consider the following questions:

- ✓ When and where does this story take place?
- ✓ How does the plot unfold in a series of episodes?
- ✓ How does the setting affect the plot? How does it affect the characters and their responses to events? How does the setting help move the plot to a resolution?

Please note that excerpts and passages in the StudySync® library and this workbook are intended as touchstones to generate interest in an author's work. The excerpts and passages do not substitute for the reading of entire texts, and StudySync® strongly recommends that students seek out and purchase the whole literary or informational work in order to experience it as the author intended. Links to online resellers are available in our digital library. In addition, complete works may be ordered through an authorized reseller by filling out and returning to StudySync® the order form enclosed in this workbook.

Reading & Writing Companion   31

SETTING

sync•skills

Skill: Setting

Reread paragraphs 10–15 from the text. Then, using the Checklist on the previous page, answer the multiple-choice questions below.

↻ YOUR TURN

1. Based on the description in paragraph 11, the reader can conclude that —

   ○ A. the story is set in a place far from water.
   ○ B. the story is set in a place that is heavily forested.
   ○ C. the story is set in a place with an obvious food source.
   ○ D. the story is set in a place covered with grass and brushland.

2. The description of Brian's thoughts in paragraphs 11–15 indicates that he feels —

   ○ A. unsure.
   ○ B. positive.
   ○ C. motivated.
   ○ D. resourceful.

3. Which paragraph best shows how the setting contributes to the conflict in the plot?

   ○ A. 10
   ○ B. 11
   ○ C. 14
   ○ D. 15

Skill:
Compare and Contrast

Use the Checklist to analyze Compare and Contrast in *Hatchet*.

••• CHECKLIST FOR COMPARE AND CONTRAST

In order to determine how to compare and contrast texts in different forms or genres, use the following steps:

- ✓ first, choose texts with similar subjects or topics

- ✓ next, identify the qualities or characteristics of each genre

- ✓ after, identify the theme in each work

- ✓ finally, analyze ways in which the texts are similar and different in the way they approach similar themes and topics

  - think about what the characters or narrators do and say
  - think about what happens as a result of the characters' or narrator's words and actions

To compare and contrast texts in different forms or genres in terms of their approaches to similar themes and topics, consider the following questions:

- ✓ How does each text approach the theme and topic? How does the form or genre of the text affect this approach?

- ✓ What are the similarities and differences in the subjects or topics of the texts I have chosen?

Please note that excerpts and passages in the StudySync® library and this workbook are intended as touchstones to generate interest in an author's work. The excerpts and passages do not substitute for the reading of entire texts, and StudySync® strongly recommends that students seek out and purchase the whole literary or informational work in order to experience it as the author intended. Links to online resellers are available in our digital library. In addition, complete works may be ordered through an authorized reseller by filling out and returning to StudySync® the order form enclosed in this workbook.

Reading & Writing Companion   33

Skill:
Compare and Contrast

Reread paragraphs 8–13 from *Hatchet* and paragraphs 17 and 18 from *Red Scarf Girl*. Then, using the Checklist on the previous page, complete the chart below to compare and contrast the passages.

↻ YOUR TURN

Inference Options	
A	Characters have to rely on their own good sense in order to solve a problem. The theme, or message, is that survival is possible if you can think clearly.
B	The main character is trapped into making a difficult decision. The genre is nonfiction.
C	The main character is alone in a strange, challenging setting. The genre is fiction.

Hatchet	Both	*Red Scarf Girl*

Close Read

Reread *Hatchet*. As you reread, complete the Skills Focus questions below. Then use your answers and annotations from the questions to help you complete the Write activity.

◎ SKILLS FOCUS

1. Identify details that Brian shares about his surroundings and explain how the evidence helps you determine the setting.

2. Identify evidence of how Brian evaluates his surroundings and explain why the details are so important to him.

3. Identify details about the setting that contribute to the conflict in *Hatchet*, and explain how these details directly affect the plot.

4. In *Red Scarf Girl*, Ji-li Jiang is pulled out of class by Communist Party officials and questioned about her family's loyalty to the Cultural Revolution. Identify details in *Red Scarf Girl* that tell you about the setting, and explain how the details help you compare this setting to the setting in *Hatchet*.

5. Identify details that demonstrate how Brian deals with the challenges he faces.

✏ WRITE

COMPARE AND CONTRAST: *Red Scarf Girl* and *Hatchet* feature young people trapped in challenging situations. In both texts, the setting provides the context for the main conflict or problem. Compare and contrast the role that the setting plays in influencing the characters and events in the two texts.

Please note that excerpts and passages in the StudySync® library and this workbook are intended as touchstones to generate interest in an author's work. The excerpts and passages do not substitute for the reading of entire texts, and StudySync® strongly recommends that students seek out and purchase the whole literary or informational work in order to experience it as the author intended. Links to online resellers are available in our digital library. In addition, complete works may be ordered through an authorized reseller by filling out and returning to StudySync® the order form enclosed in this workbook.

Reading & Writing Companion   **35**

The Magic Marker Mystery

DRAMA
René Saldaña, Jr.
2013

Introduction

Author René Saldaña, Jr. draws from both his Texas upbringing and his past as a middle-school teacher to create characters like the young sleuth Mickey Rangel. In this short play, Mickey is employed by his principal in order to find out who is behind some graffiti that has recently turned up at the school. Mickey is forced to use his detective skills, as well as a recent English class lesson on homophones, to figure out which of his classmates has been defacing

"I've got to do the job right, even if it means going against my gut instinct."

NOTES

Characters

Mickey Rangel
Principal Abrego
Bucho
Joe
Belinda
Johnny

Setting

A middle school in a Midwestern suburb

1 **ACT ONE:** PRINCIPAL ABREGO's office. The principal is sitting at a large wooden desk. Sunlight streams in from two large windows to her right.

2 PRINCIPAL ABREGO (*buzzes phone*): Angie, can you please send Mickey in now?

3 (*door opens, MICKEY RANGEL reluctantly walks in*)

4 PRINCIPAL ABREGO (*shuffling papers, and without looking at MICKEY*): Won't you have a seat, Mr. Rangel? I'll be just a moment. (*continues shuffling papers for a couple more seconds, then sets them in order and places them on the desk*) So, (*looks up at MICKEY finally*) you must be wondering why I've called you to my office?

5 MICKEY (*leg shaking, swallows hard*): Sort of. I've been going over in my head what I could have possibly done to **merit** being summoned to the principal's office, and though there is that spitball **incident** from this morning on the bus, it was only this morning and mostly between my brother Ricky and me, so word couldn't have gotten to you this quickly, and even if it had, my actions weren't so bad that. . .(*MICKEY notices PRINCIPAL ABREGO has reached for a pen to begin taking notes, and that she also has the traces of a smile on her face.*) I mean, yes, ma'am, I am wondering why you would call me here.

Skill: Dramatic Elements and Structure

I know that this is a drama about a student, and this scene shows me that the play takes place at school because he's talking to the principal.

Mickey seems nervous in this setting, but the principal is smiling. I wonder if Mickey is in trouble or not, and what will happen next...

6 PRINCIPAL ABREGO: Well. . .never mind about the, uh, spitball episode, at least for now. (*raises an eyebrow, then smiles*) As to why I've asked you to my office this morning, Mr Rangel—may I call you Mickey?

7 MICKEY: Certainly, ma'am.

8 PRINCIPAL ABREGO: I'm sure you've seen the graffiti marring our walls lately. The substance of the messages, mostly aimed at me, is fairly harmless. I'm a principal, so I've had to grow a thick skin over the years. What is bothersome beyond belief, though, is that someone thinks so very little of our school that they would show such disrespect. (*shakes her head*)

Graffiti

9 MICKEY: Mrs. Abrego, you don't think that I. . .?

10 PRINCIPAL ABREGO: Oh, goodness, no, Mickey. I'm sorry I haven't made myself clear. No, I don't think for a second you have anything to do with this.

11 MICKEY (*sighs in relief*): So then why am I here, if you don't mind me asking?

12 PRINCIPAL ABREGO: Am I right in saying you're sort of a detective, young though you are?

13 MICKEY: Actually, Mrs. Abrego, I'm the real deal. I took the required online courses to earn my degree. I've got a framed diploma at home to prove it. (*pulls wallet from back pocket, rifles through it as though in search of something*) I also carry my official P.I. ID card. P.I.—that stands for *private investigator*. You want to see it? (*finds it and offers it to PRINCIPAL ABREGO*)

14 PRINCIPAL ABREGO (*takes it from MICKEY and studies it briefly, then returns it*): That's very impressive, Mickey.

15 MICKEY: Thank you, ma'am. But I still don't understand why I'm here.

16 PRINCIPAL ABREGO: Mickey, I'll be frank with you: I'm in a bit of a sticky situation. (*pushes aside a few papers on her desk, stands, and walks to the window overlooking the playground*) Take a look out the window with me and tell me what you see.

17 MICKEY: Yes, ma'am. (*rises, makes his way around the desk, and walks over to the window*)

18 PRINCIPAL ABREGO: Can you read it from here?

Skill: Dramatic Elements and Structure

Principal Abrego didn't call Mickey to her office because he's in trouble. She's asking for his help! She must want him to use his detective skills to find the person responsible for the graffiti.

19   MICKEY (*reads aloud*): "Our Principle's no pal of nobodies!" Interesting spelling and punctuation choices this Magic Marker Mischief Maker has made.

20   PRINCIPAL ABREGO: You noticed? Good. Yes, it should read "principal," ending in "PAL," not "PLE." Major difference.

21   MICKEY: Yes, and "nobody" is spelled as though it were plural, ending in "-dies," though it should not be a plural. And is that a small letter "B" at the bottom right corner, like a signature?

22   PRINCIPAL ABREGO: You caught that too? Most impressive Mickey.

23   MICKEY (*smiles*): Thanks, ma'am.

24   PRINCIPAL ABREGO: I also got this anonymous email this morning right as I turned on my computer. The author claims to be an eye-witness to the wrongdoing. What do you make of it? (*hands MICKEY the sheet of paper*)

25   MICKEY (*reads the email*): Hmmmm. Incriminating, to say the least. So the letter "B" on the wall would make sense. Based on these two clues, all fingers point to Bucho being our mischief maker.

26   PRINCIPAL ABREGO: Yes, that's what I thought. But here's the thing, Mickey. I confronted him with this evidence, and he denies having anything to do with marking up our walls. Believe it or not, tough though he comes across, he was nearly in tears.

27   MICKEY: Ma'am, I'm not so sure you should be telling me this. Isn't there some kind of student-principal privilege?

28   PRINCIPAL ABREGO: Normally, yes, but he gave me permission to discuss this whole matter with you, every bit of it.

29   MICKEY: Wait—what? You mean he told you it was okay to talk to me about this? Why would he do that?

30   PRINCIPAL ABREGO: Mickey, Bucho was so **adamant** that he wasn't the **culprit** that he recommended I bring you in on the case. He's the one who told me you were a detective.

31   MICKEY: He said that?

32   PRINCIPAL ABREGO: Are you surprised?

33   MICKEY: Yes, ma'am. You might not know this about us, but he and I are not the best of friends. To be honest, Mrs. Abrego, he's a bit of a bully.

34   PRINCIPAL ABREGO: That he is. But he and I have been trying to work on that part of his life. In the last few months he's made some great strides, and so

when I got this email and put it together with the so-called signature, it was easy to jump to conclusions. And this is where you come in, Mickey. I was filled with indecision about what I should do about this, but now I think I've found an answer. I need you to find out who is to blame for the graffiti. Can you help me?

35   MICKEY: You can count on me. Mickey Rangel is on the case.

36   PRINCIPAL ABREGO: Good. Whatever you need, please don't hesitate to ask. In fact, think of me as your benefactor.

37   **ACT TWO, SCENE 1:** First lunch period. MICKEY is eating at a table in the school cafeteria; with him are his friends BELINDA and JOHNNY. JOE, another student, is sitting alone at a nearby table, eavesdropping on MICKEY and friends.

38   BELINDA: You know, Mickey, I'm not the only one who thinks this school would be a better place without that bully, Bucho. I can't even count the multitude of times he's knocked my book bag off my shoulder, as if that were some kind of big joke. (*BELINDA looks reflective for a moment.*) Come to think of it, though, he's walked past me a couple of times the past few weeks and nothing's happened.

39   JOHNNY: Well, all I can say is, I thought it was just a myth about the school bully taking your lunch, but it's true. He hasn't done it for a while, but I still bring rice cakes and celery sticks for lunch because it's the only stuff he won't try and steal from me.

40   MICKEY: Yeah, but what kind of a detective would I be if I'm **presuming** a kid is guilty instead of presuming he's innocent? Not a very good one. And Principal Abrego has been having talks with him, and she claims he's really trying hard to be less of a bully lately.

41   JOHNNY: You might be right about that, but I'd be able to bring a sandwich for lunch again if you did assume he's guilty and found the proof of it. I mean, it's Bucho we're talking about here.

42   *JOE looks over his shoulder at MICKEY and friends, smiles to himself and rubs his hands as if he's won a game of chess; he coughs into his fist: "Bucho's a loser!")*

43   MICKEY: (*turns to JOE*) I'm sorry; did you say something, Joe?

44   JOE: Who, me? Nope. You must be hearing things.

45   MICKEY: Maybe, Joe. But I thought I heard you say, "Bucho's a loser."

46   JOE: I said no such thing. Like I told you, Mickey, you must be hearing things. Get your ears checked.

Copyright © BookheadEd Learning, LLC

NOTES

47 MICKEY: You're probably right. (*turns back to his friends, thinks for a split second, then turns back to JOE*) Say, Joe, why are you eating all alone? Don't you normally eat lunch with Bucho? He is your best friend, isn't he?

48 JOE: Yeah, well. . . (*JOE scans the room as if looking for somebody.*) Maybe he is and maybe he isn't. Anyway, I'll bet he's probably out marking up a wall somewhere. And I think your pals here are right: Bucho's your man. What is it they say about leopards and their dots?

49 MICKEY: Spots, Joe, you mean "spots."

50 JOE: Yeah, whatever. But like I'm saying, he's so dumb he's even signing his tags with a "B" right? (*JOE stands up and takes his tray off the table.*)

51 MICKEY: Funny way to talk about your best friend. (*JOE gives MICKEY a hard look and then departs without saying anything.*)

52 MICKEY (*turns back to his friends, thinks for a couple short beats*): Anyhow, I'd like to see Bucho gone, too, but I made a promise, Johnny. It's not so simple for me. I've got to do the job right, even if it means going against my gut instinct.

53 BELINDA: So what are you saying, Mickey? You think he's innocent? If you ask a hundred kids who they think is leaving those messages around the school, a hundred of them will say it's got to be Bucho. Who else would it be? He's probably not bullying people as much now because he has a new endeavor—writing graffiti.

54 MICKEY: But a survey isn't evidence.

55 JOHNNY: But you do have evidence, don't you? You said the principal showed you the email in which someone claimed to have seen Bucho in action, writing on the wall.

56 MICKEY: That's circumstantial. Not in the least incriminating without anything else of substance.

57 BELINDA: So, what about the letter "B" the culprit has left behind as a kind of signature—is Joe lying about that?

58 MICKEY: Also circumstantial. I mean, if a "B" is all we've got, who's to say it doesn't stand for "Belinda"? (*BELINDA looks as though she's been accused.*) Don't get me wrong—I'm not saying it's you, I'm saying a "B" is not enough to prove a guy's guilt.

59 BELINDA: Are you saying you're not willing to stand with me—(*looks at JOHNNY*) with us—and instead you're going to side with Bucho?

60 MICKEY: That's not it at all. What I'm saying is that I've got to do this the right way. I would think you'd understand that my work and doing it right are important to me.

61 BELINDA: No, Mickey. There's nothing "right" about Bucho's ugly behavior all these years. Do you really think a few weeks of acting nice can erase years of mean behavior? Whatever! It's up to you to do the right thing. (*BELINDA stands suddenly and walks away.*)

62 MICKEY: Belinda just doesn't get it, Johnny. I'm a detective; I took an oath to dig and dig until I find the truth, even if I don't like the outcome. I'm not saying it's not Bucho, it's just that I need extensive evidence to prove that it is him. (*he pauses, then looks at JOHNNY*) Besides, putting the blame on Bucho without evidence is just another form of bullying, isn't it? Only this time, we'd be the bullies. (*JOHNNY looks thoughtful and walks away.*)

63 **ACT TWO, SCENE 2:** Second lunch period. MICKEY is sitting alone, deep in thought, unaware that the bell has rung. Suddenly, BUCHO looms in front of MICKEY.

64 BUCHO: Hey, Mickey. . .I imagine Mrs. A told you the story. Somebody's trying to frame me for all this graffiti, and I bet you won't believe me, but it wasn't me. And you're the only one I trust to uncover the truth.

65 MICKEY: I told Mrs. A I would, so I'm going to help any way I can.

66 BUCHO: Ok, bro. Say, you going to eat that? (*Before MICKEY can answer, BUCHO reaches for MICKEY's brownie and swallows it in one bite; then he walks away from the table with his own tray in hand.*)

67 MICKEY: Hey, Bucho. (*BUCHO turns*) How do you spell "principal"? As in Mrs. Abrego, the school's big cheese?

68 BUCHO: First, are you kidding? What other kind of principal is there? Second, are you making fun of me? Because if you are. . .(*BUCHO shakes a fist at MICKEY, but then he thinks better of it and puts his hand down.*)

69 MICKEY: So spell it.

70 BUCHO (*scowling, exaggerating his pronunciation*): P-R-I-N-C-I-P-A-L. As in, Mrs. Abrego is our PAL. Satisfied?

71 MICKEY: Yup. (*BUCHO walks away, this time for good.*)

72 **ACT THREE:** Outside, the school playground, where PRINCIPAL ABREGO, BUCHO, and OTHERS have gathered in front of the site of the latest graffiti. BELINDA stands against a wall nearby. MICKEY enters from stage right.

73 PRINCIPAL ABREGO: There you are, Mickey. As you can see, I've asked Bucho to join us, as you requested. Can we get started now? (*Beyond PRINCIPAL ABREGO and BUCHO are a multitude of kids playing different games. Among them are JOE, who is noticeably nervous and keeping a careful eye on the developments from a safe distance, and BELINDA, who is standing against a wall nearby.*)

74 MICKEY: Sure thing. First of all, you were right. In the case of The Magic Marker Mischief Maker, someone other than Bucho is responsible for this graffiti. My first clue was the curious spelling. Only two weeks ago in English we were studying homophones. One set of words we were asked to learn included the "principal/principle" set.

75 BUCHO: Yeah, that's right. Miss Garza gave us a trick to remember how to spell it: "Mrs. Abrego, the principal, is our pal." (*BUCHO looks at MICKEY.*) Like I told you at lunch.

76 MICKEY: Exactly, but at lunch you also said, "What other kind of "principal" is there?" when in fact there are two. You had no clue about the other spelling; P-R-I-N-C-I-P-L-E, which means "a high standard that guides one's actions and reactions." You must've been looking at the insides of your eyelids when Miss Garza was going over that one.

77 BUCHO: Watch yourself.

78 PRINCIPAL ABREGO: No, watch yourself, Bernard. Mickey's trying to help, so help yourself by minding your temper.

79 BUCHO: Yes, ma'am.

80 MICKEY: *Bernard?* Really?

81 (*BUCHO scowls and tentatively takes a step in MICKEY's direction, but then he steps back.*)

82 MICKEY: Allow me to go on. If you don't know how to spell both words, much less that there are two variations, then you couldn't have written this graffiti. (*waves a hand at the wall*) This tells me that our culprit is also studying vocabulary in Miss Garza's class, though it's obvious he's not learning.

83 BUCHO: Well, spit it out: if it wasn't me, then who?

84 MICKEY: Hey, Joe, can you come here?

85 JOE (*walks over*): What's up, man? (*He refuses to acknowledge BUCHO.*)

86 MICKEY: Can you spell the word "principal" for us, as in Mrs. Abrego, our school's principal? You know, like we were supposed to have learned in Miss Garza's class.

87 JOE: Are you kidding me?

88 PRINCIPAL ABREGO: Mickey?

89 MICKEY: Ma'am? (*motions as though for support from MRS. ABREGO*)

90 PRINCIPAL ABREGO: Okay, then. Go on, Joe, do as he says.

91 JOE (*puffs his chest out proudly*): P-R-I-N-C-I-P-L-E, "principle," as in "The last thing I want is to be sent to the principle's office." Satisfied?

92 MICKEY: Quite.

93 PRINCIPAL ABREGO: Quite indeed. (*speaking to JOE*) Young man, though it's the last thing you want to do, you will follow me to my office. (*The two leave, though MRS. ABREGO does put an arm around JOE's shoulders indicating she will want to "work with" him in the same way she's been working with BUCHO.*)

94 BUCHO: Mickey, you did it! You proved my innocence!

95 MICKEY: I also proved you need to pay more attention in class.

96 BUCHO (*looks to make sure MRS. ABREGO is out of sight before taking a menacing step toward MICKEY*): Why, I oughta…

Used with permission of McGraw-Hill Education.

First Read

Read *The Magic Marker Mystery*. After you read, complete the Think Questions below.

1. How does Bucho's past behavior make him an easy target for the real graffiti artist? Cite textual evidence from the selection to support your answer.

2. Write two to three sentences describing how Bucho reacts to being the target of bullying. Cite textual evidence from the selection to support your answer.

3. The stage directions for Act Three say that Belinda stands "against a wall nearby." How would you explain Belinda's behavior during this scene? Cite textual evidence from the selection to support your answer.

4. Find the word **culprit** in paragraph 30 of *The Magic Marker Mystery*. Use context clues in the surrounding sentences, as well as the sentence in which the word appears, to determine the word's meaning. Write your definition here and identify clues that helped you figure out its meaning.

5. Use context clues to determine the meaning of **presuming** as it is used in paragraph 40 of *The Magic Marker Mystery*. Write your definition here and identify clues that helped you figure out its meaning. Then check the meaning in a dictionary.

Please note that excerpts and passages in the StudySync® library and this workbook are intended as touchstones to generate interest in an author's work. The excerpts and passages do not substitute for the reading of entire texts, and StudySync® strongly recommends that students seek out and purchase the whole literary or informational work in order to experience it as the author intended. Links to online resellers are available in our digital library. In addition, complete works may be ordered through an authorized reseller by filling out and returning to StudySync® the order form enclosed in this workbook.

Reading & Writing
Companion

45

Skill: Dramatic Elements and Structure

Use the Checklist to analyze Dramatic Elements and Structure in *The Magic Marker Mystery*. Refer to the sample student annotations about Dramatic Elements and Structure in the text.

••• CHECKLIST FOR DRAMATIC ELEMENTS AND STRUCTURE

In order to identify the dramatic elements and structure of a play, note the following:

✓ the order of acts and scenes in the play

✓ what happens in each act and scene

✓ how the acts and scenes work together to develop the plot

✓ the setting of the play and how it changes by act and scene

✓ the information in stage directions, including lighting, sound, and set, as well as details about characters, including exits and entrances

To analyze how a particular scene fits into the overall structure of a text and contributes to the development of the theme, setting, or plot, consider the following questions:

✓ When does this particular scene appear?

✓ How does this scene fit into the overall structure of the text?

✓ How do setting, characters, and other elements in the scene contribute to the development of the plot?

✓ What does the scene contribute to the theme or message of the drama?

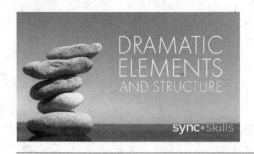

Skill: Dramatic Elements and Structure

Reread paragraphs 75–92 from Act Three of *The Magic Marker Mystery*. Then, using the Checklist on the previous page, answer the multiple-choice questions below.

🔁 YOUR TURN

1. Why is mentioning the conversation in the lunchroom (paragraphs 75–76) important to the plot?

   ○ A. Mickey understands that Bucho never pays attention in class.

   ○ B. Mickey is able to grasp that Bucho is not the guilty party.

   ○ C. Bucho realizes that Mickey is attempting to make fun of him.

   ○ D. Bucho admires Mickey's thorough detective skills.

2. What does the dialogue exchanged between Mickey and Principal Abrego in paragraphs 88–90 reveal about the plot?

   ○ A. Principal Abrego is upset with Mickey for overstepping his authority in the situation.

   ○ B. Principal Abrego shows amazement at Mickey's detective skills.

   ○ C. Mickey checks in with Principal Abrego when he needs help solving the case.

   ○ D. Mickey is disappointed that Principal Abrego doesn't trust him to solve the case.

3. In the drama, Mickey asks Joe to spell the word "principal." What does the dialogue exchanged between Mickey and Joe in paragraphs 84–92 reveal about the plot?

   ○ A. Joe admires Miss Garza's clever vocabulary tricks.

   ○ B. Joe makes fun of Mickey for being called to the principal's office.

   ○ C. Joe is a top vocabulary student in Miss Garza's class.

   ○ D. Joe is the culprit because this spelling matches the graffiti.

Please note that excerpts and passages in the StudySync® library and this workbook are intended as touchstones to generate interest in an author's work. The excerpts and passages do not substitute for the reading of entire texts, and StudySync® strongly recommends that students seek out and purchase the whole literary or informational work in order to experience it as the author intended. Links to online resellers are available in our digital library. In addition, complete works may be ordered through an authorized reseller by filling out and returning to StudySync® the order form enclosed in this workbook.

Reading & Writing
Companion

47

Close Read

Reread *The Magic Marker Mystery*. As you reread, complete the Skills Focus questions below. Then use your answers and annotations from the questions to help you complete the Write activity.

◎ SKILLS FOCUS

1. Identify a scene or line of dialogue in Act 1 that helps to develop or move the plot forward.

2. Identify how the other characters feel about Bucho in Act Two, Scene 1.

3. Identify lines of dialogue or stage directions that show Bucho's attempt to change from being a bully.

4. Think about the challenges the characters face in *The Magic Marker Mystery*. Identify the challenges and what the characters choose to do about it.

✎ WRITE

LITERARY ANALYSIS: Think about how the playwright uses specific scenes to develop the plot. How would Act Three of *The Magic Marker Mystery* be different if it were told from Joe's perspective? In your response, indicate how this would affect the structure of the play as a whole. Support your writing with specific evidence from the text.

Scout's Honor

FICTION
Avi
1996

Introduction

Avi is the pen name of Edward Irving Wortis (b. 1937), the Newbery Medal-winning author of more than 75 books for children and young adults. Avi was born and raised in New York City, and his childhood and adolescence were an inspiration for many of his stories and books. "Scout's Honor," presented here, is the humorous story of a nine-year-old boy and his Boy Scout friends who set out to the New Jersey "wilderness" to prove their toughness. Avi's body of work spans many genres, from historical fiction to graphic novels. Yet his stories and books are united by their relatable and evocative depictions of young people in

"The way they agreed made me nervous. Now I really was going to have to be tough."

Skill: Story Structure

These sentences tell me that this story will be about an overnight camping adventure. It will be a new experience for the narrator since he will be leaving Brooklyn for the first time, without adult supervision.

This sentence in paragraph 2 tells me that the setting plays an important role in the story. It will probably have an effect on what happens to the boys because the narrator isn't used to the country.

1   Back in 1946, when I was nine, I worried that I wasn't tough enough. That's why I became a Boy Scout. Scouting, I thought, would make a man of me. It didn't take long to reach Tenderfoot rank. You got that for joining. To move up to Second Class, however, you had to meet three requirements. Scout Spirit and Scout Participation had been cinchy. The third requirement, Scout Craft, meant I had to go on an overnight hike in the *country*. In other words, I had to leave Brooklyn, on my own, for the first time in my life.

2   Since I grew up in Brooklyn in the 1940s, the only grass I knew was in Ebbets Field where the Dodgers played. Otherwise, my world was made of slate pavements, streets of asphalt (or cobblestone), and skies full of tall buildings. The only thing "country" was a puny pin oak tree at our curb, which was noticed, mostly, by dogs.

3   I asked Scoutmaster Brenkman where I could find some country. Now, whenever I saw Mr. Brenkman, who was a church pastor, he was dressed in either church black or Scout khaki. When he wore black, he'd warn us against hellfire. When he wore khaki, he'd teach us how to build fires.

4   "Country," Scoutmaster Brenkman said in answer to my question, "is anywhere that has lots of trees and is not the city. Many boys camp in the Palisades."

5   "Where's that?"

6   "Just north of the city. It's a park in Jersey."

7   "Isn't that a zillion miles from here?"

8   "Take the subway to the George Washington Bridge, then hike across."

9   I thought for a moment, then asked, "How do I prove I went?"

10 Mr. Brenkman looked deeply shocked. "You wouldn't *lie*, would you? What about Scout's honor?"

11 "Yes, sir," I replied meekly.

Reading & Writing Companion

12 My two best friends were Philip Hossfender, whom we nicknamed Horse, and Richard Macht, called Max because we were not great spellers. They were also Scouts, Tenderfoots like me.

13 Horse was a skinny little kid about half my size whose way of arguing was to ball up his fist and say, "Are you saying. . .?" in a threatening tone.

14 Max was on the pudgy side, but he could talk his way out of a locked room. More importantly, he always seemed to have pocket money, which gave his talk real power.

15 I wasn't sure why, but being best friends meant we were rivals too. One of the reasons for my wanting to be tougher was a feeling that Horse was a lot tougher than I was, and that Max was a little tougher.

16 "I'm going camping in the Palisades next weekend," I casually informed them.

17 "How come?" Max challenged.

18 "Scout Craft," I replied.

19 "Oh, *that,*" Horse said with a shrug.

20 "Look," I said, "I don't know about you, but I don't intend to be a Tenderfoot all my life. Anyway, doing stuff in the city is for sissies. Scouting is real camping. Besides, I like roughing it."

21 "You saying I don't?" Horse snapped.

22 "I'm not saying nothing," I said.

23 They considered my idea. Finally, Horse said, "Yeah, well, I was going to do that, but I didn't think you guys were ready for it."

24 "I've been ready for *years*," Max protested.

25 "Then we're going, right?" I said.

26 They looked around at me. "If you can do it, I can do it," Max said.

27 "Yeah," Horse said thoughtfully.

28 The way they agreed made me nervous. Now I really was going to have to be tough.

29 We informed our folks that we were going camping overnight (which was true) and that the Scoutmaster was going with us—which was a lie. We did remember what Mr. Brenkman said about honesty, but we were baseball fans too, and since we were prepared to follow Scout law—being loyal, helpful, friendly, **courteous,** kind, obedient, cheerful, thrifty, brave, clean *and* reverent—we figured a 900 batting average was not bad.

NOTES

Skill:
Plot

These early paragraphs tell me that the plot will involve friends who are trying to prove they're tough. I think it is the inciting incident because it seems to set up the rest of the story.

30   So Saturday morning we met at the High Street subway station. I got there first. Stuffed in my dad's army surplus knapsack was a blanket, a pillow, and a paper bag with three white-bread peanut-butter-and-jelly sandwiches—that is, lunch, supper, and Sunday breakfast. My pockets were full of stick matches. I had an old flashlight, and since I lived by the Scout motto—Be Prepared—I had brought along an umbrella. Finally, being a serious reader, I had the latest Marvel Family comics.

31   Horse arrived next, his arms barely managing to hold on to a mattress that seemed twice his size. As for food, he had four cans of beans jammed into his pockets.

32   Max came last. He was lugging a new knapsack that contained a cast-iron frying pan, a packet of hot dogs, and a box of saltine crackers—plus two bottles. One bottle was mustard, the other, celery soda. He also had a bag of Tootsie Rolls and a shiny hatchet. "To build a lean-to," he explained.

33   Max's prize **possession,** however, was an official Scout compass. "It's really swell," he told us. "You can't ever get lost with it. Got it at the Scout store."

34   "I hate that place," Horse informed us. "It's all new. Nothing real."

35   "This compass is real," Max retorted. "Points north all the time. You can get cheaper ones, but they point all different directions."

36   "What's so great about the north?" Horse said.

37   "That's always the way to go," Max insisted.

38   "Says who?" I demanded.

39   "Mr. Brenkman, dummy," Horse cried. "Anyway, there's always an arrow on maps pointing the way north."

40   "Cowboys live out west," I reminded them. They didn't care.

41   On the subway platform, we realized we did not know which station we were heading for. To find out, we studied the system map, which looked like a noodle factory hit by a bomb. The place we wanted to go (north) was at the top of the map, so I had to hoist Horse onto my shoulders for a closer look. Since he refused to let go of his mattress—or the tin cans in his pockets—it wasn't easy. I asked him—in a kindly fashion—to put the mattress down.

42   No sooner did he find the station—168th Street—than our train arrived. We rushed on, only to have Horse scream, "My mattress!" He had left it on the platform. Just before the doors shut, he and I leaped off. Max, however, remained on the train. Helplessly, we watched as his horror-stricken face slid away from us. "Wait at the next station!" I bellowed. "Don't move!"

Copyright © BookheadEd Learning, LLC

43   The next train took forever to come. Then it took even longer to get to the next stop. There was Max. All around him—like fake snow in a glass ball—were crumbs. He'd been so nervous he had eaten all his crackers.

44   "Didn't that make you thirsty?"

45   "I drank my soda."

46   I noticed streaks down his cheeks. Horse noticed them too. "You been crying?" he asked.

47   "Naw," Max said. "There was this water dripping from the tunnel roof. But, you said don't move, right? Well, I was just being obedient."

48   By the time we got on the next train—with all our possessions—we had been traveling for an hour. But we had managed to go only one stop.

49   During the ride, I got hungry. I pulled out one of my sandwiches. With the jelly soaked through the bread, it looked like a limp scab.

50   Horse, **envious,** complained *he* was getting hungry.

51   "Eat some of your canned beans," I suggested.

52   He got out one can without ripping his pocket too badly. Then his face took on a mournful look.

53   "What's the matter?" I asked.

54   "Forgot to bring a can opener."

55   Max said, "In the old days, people opened cans with their teeth."

56   "You saying my teeth aren't strong?"

57   "I'm just talking about history!"

58   "You saying I don't know history?"

59   Always kind, I plopped half my sandwich into Horse's hand. He squashed it into his mouth and was quiet for the next fifteen minutes. It proved something I'd always believed: The best way to stop arguments is to get people to eat peanut butter sandwiches. They can't talk.

60   Then we became so **absorbed** in our Marvel Family comics we missed our station. We got to it only by coming back the other way. When we reached street level, the sky was dark.

61   "I knew it," Max announced. "It's going to rain."

Skill:
Plot

I see that the boys' adventure is going from bad to worse. Max began by being brave, but now I see that he has been crying. This is the conflict, and it suggests to me that there will be more challenges ahead before a resolution is reached.

Please note that excerpts and passages in the StudySync® library and this workbook are intended as touchstones to generate interest in an author's work. The excerpts and passages do not substitute for the reading of entire texts, and StudySync® strongly recommends that students seek out and purchase the whole literary or informational work in order to experience it as the author intended. Links to online resellers are available in our digital library. In addition, complete works may be ordered through an authorized reseller by filling out and returning to StudySync® the order form enclosed in this workbook.

Reading & Writing
Companion

53

NOTES

62   "Don't worry," Horse said. "New Jersey is a whole other state. It probably won't be raining there."

63   "I brought an umbrella," I said smugly, though I wanted it to sound helpful.

64   As we marched down 168th Street, heading for the George Washington Bridge, we looked like European war refugees. Every few paces, Horse cried, "Hold it!" and adjusted his arms around his mattress. Each time we paused, Max pulled out his compass, peered at it, then announced, "Heading north!"

65   I said, "The bridge goes from east to west."

66   "Maybe the bridge does," Max insisted with a show of his compass, "but guaranteed, *we* are going north."

67   About then, the heel of my left foot, encased in a heavy rubber boot over an earth-crushing Buster Brown shoe, started to get sore. Things weren't going as I had hoped. Cheerfully, I tried to ignore the pain.

68   The closer we drew to the bridge, the more **immense** it seemed. And the clouds had become so thick, you couldn't see the top of the far side.

69   Max eyed the bridge with deep suspicion. "I'm not so sure we should go," he said.

70   "Why?"

71   "Maybe it doesn't have another side."

72   We looked at him.

73   "No, seriously," Max explained, "they could have taken the Jersey side away, you know, for repairs."

74   "Cars are going across," I pointed out.

75   "They could be dropping off," he suggested.

76   "You would hear them splash," Horse argued.

77   "I'm going," I said. Trying to look brave, I started off on my own. My bravery didn't last for long. The walkway was narrow. When I looked down, I saw only fog. I could feel the bridge tremble and sway. It wasn't long before I was convinced the bridge was about to collapse. Then a ray of hope struck me: Maybe the other guys had chickened out. If they had, I could quit because of *them*. I glanced back. My heart sank. They were coming.

78   After they caught up, Horse looked me in the eye and said, "If this bridge falls, I'm going to kill you."

Skill: Story Structure

I think the boys are trying to prove that they're tough. I think this event is important to the theme since the narrator wants to prove he's brave in front of his friends. I wonder if this attitude will continue throughout the whole story.

NOTES

79 A quarter of a mile farther across, I gazed around. We were completely fogged in.

80 "I think we're lost," I announced.

81 "What do we do?" Horse whispered. His voice was jagged with panic. That made me feel better.

82 "Don't worry," Max said. "I've got my compass." He pulled it out. "North is that way," he said, pointing in the direction we had been going.

83 Horse said, "You sure?"

84 "A Scout compass never lies," Max insisted.

85 "*We* lied," I reminded him.

86 "Yeah, but this is an *official* Scout compass," Max returned loyally.

87 "Come on," Max said and marched forward. Horse and I followed. In moments, we crossed a metal bar on the walkway. On one side, a sign proclaimed: NEW YORK; on the other, it said: NEW JERSEY.

88 "Holy smoke," Horse said with reverence as he straddled the bar. "Talk about being tough. We're in two states at the same time."

89 It began to rain. Max said, "Maybe it'll keep us clean."

90 "You saying I'm not clean?" Horse shot back.

91 Ever friendly, I put up my umbrella.

92 We went on—Max on one side, Horse on the other, me in the middle—trying to avoid the growing puddles. After a while, Max said, "Would you move the umbrella? Rain is coming down my neck."

93 "We're supposed to be roughing it," I said.

94 "Being in the middle isn't roughing it," Horse reminded me.

95 I folded the umbrella up so we could all get soaked equally.

96 "Hey!" I cried. "Look!" Staring up ahead, I could make out tollbooths and the dim outlines of buildings.

97 "Last one off the bridge is a rotten egg!" Horse shouted and began to run. The next second, he tripped and took off like an F-36 fighter plane. Unfortunately, he landed like a Hell-cat dive-bomber as his mattress unspooled before him and then slammed into a big puddle.

98 Max and I ran to help. Horse was damp. His mattress was soaked. When he tried to roll it up, water cascaded like Niagara Falls.

99 "Better leave it," Max said.

100 "It's what I sleep on at home," Horse said as he slung the soaking, dripping mass over his shoulder.

101 When we got off the bridge, we were in a small plaza. To the left was the roadway, full of roaring cars. In front of us, aside from the highway, there was nothing but buildings. Only to the right were there trees.

102 "North is that way," Max said, pointing toward the trees. We set off.

103 "How come you're limping?" Horse asked me. My foot *was* killing me. All I said, though, was, "How come you keep rubbing your arm?"

104 "I'm keeping the blood moving."

105 We **approached** a grove of trees. "Wow," Horse exclaimed. "Country." But as we drew closer, what we found were discarded cans, bottles, and newspapers—plus an old mattress spring.

106 "Hey," Max cried, sounding relieved, "this is just like Brooklyn."

107 I said, "Let's find a decent place, make camp, and eat."

108 It was hard to find a campsite that didn't have junk. The growing dark didn't help. We had to settle for the place that had the least amount of garbage.

109 Max said, "If we build a lean-to, it'll keep us out of the rain." He and Horse went a short distance with the hatchet.

110 Seeing a tree they wanted, Max whacked at it. The hatchet bounced right out of his hand. There was not even a dent in the tree. Horse retrieved the hatchet and checked the blade. "Dull," he said.

111 "Think I'm going to carry something sharp and cut myself?" Max protested. They contented themselves with picking up branches.

112 I went in search of firewood, but everything was wet. When I finally gathered some twigs and tried to light them, the only thing that burned was my fingers.

113 Meanwhile, Horse and Max used their branches to build a lean-to directly over me. After many collapses—which didn't help my work—they finally got the branches to stand in a shaky sort of way.

114 "Uh-oh," Horse said. "We forgot to bring something for a cover."

115 Max eyed me. "Didn't you say you brought a blanket?"

NOTES

116   "No way!" I cried.

117   "All in favor of using the blanket!"

118   Horse and Max both cried, "Aye."

119   Only after I built up a mound of partially burned match sticks and lit *them*, did I get the fire going. It proved that where there's smoke there doesn't have to be much fire. The guys meanwhile draped my blanket over their branch construction. It collapsed twice.

120   About an hour after our arrival, the three of us were gathered inside the tiny space. There was a small fire, but more light came from my flickering flashlight.

121   "No more rain," Horse said with pride.

122   "Just smoke," I said, rubbing my stinging eyes.

123   "We need a vent hole," Horse pointed out.

124   "I could cut it with the hatchet," Max said.

125   "It's my mother's favorite blanket."

126   "And you took it?" Max said.

127   I nodded.

128   "You *are* tough," Horse said.

129   Besides having too much smoke in our eyes and being wet, tired, and in pain, we were starving. I almost said something about giving up, but as far as I could see, the other guys were still tough.

130   Max put his frying pan atop my smoldering smoke. After dumping in the entire contents of his mustard bottle, he threw in the franks. Meanwhile, I bolted down my last sandwich.

131   "What am I going to eat?" Horse suddenly said.

132   "Your beans," I reminded him.

133   Max offered up his hatchet. "Here. Just chop off the top end of the can."

134   "Oh, right," Horse said. He selected a can, set it in front of him, levered himself onto his knees, then swung down—hard. There was an explosion. For a stunned moment, we just sat there, hands, face, and clothing dripping with beans.

135 Suddenly Max shouted, "Food fight! Food fight!" and began to paw the stuff off and fling it around.

136 Having a food fight in a cafeteria is one thing. Having one in the middle of a soaking wet lean-to with cold beans during a dark, wet New Jersey night is another. In seconds, the lean-to was down, the fire kicked over, and Max's frankfurters dumped on the ground.

137 "The food!" Max screamed, and began to snatch up the franks. Coated with mustard, dirt, grass, and leaves, they looked positively prehistoric. Still, we wiped the franks clean on our pants then ate them—the franks, that is. Afterward, we picked beans off each other's clothes—the way monkeys help friends get rid of lice.

138 For dessert, Max shared some Tootsie Rolls. After Horse swallowed his sixteenth piece, he announced, "I don't feel so good."

139 The thought of his getting sick was too much. "Let's go home," I said, ashamed to look at the others. To my surprise—and relief—nobody objected.

140 Wet and cold, our way lit by my fast-fading flashlight, we gathered our belongings—most of them, anyway. As we made our way back over the bridge, gusts of wind-blown rain pummeled us until I felt like a used-up punching bag. By the time we got to the subway station, my legs were melting fast. The other guys looked bad too. Other riders moved away from us. One of them murmured, "Juvenile delinquents." To cheer us up, I got out my comic books, but they had congealed into a lump of red, white, and blue pulp.

141 With the subways running slow, it took hours to get home. When we emerged from the High Street Station, it was close to midnight.

142 Before we split up to go to our own homes, we just stood there on a street corner, embarrassed, trying to figure out how to end the day gracefully. I was the one who said, "Okay, I admit it. I'm not as tough as you guys. I gave up first."

143 Max shook his head. "Naw. I wanted to quit, but I wasn't tough enough to do it." He looked to Horse.

144 Horse made a fist. "You saying I'm the one who's tough?" he demanded. "I hate roughing it!"

145 "Me too," I said quickly.

146 "Same for me," Max said.

147 Horse said, "Only thing is, we just have to promise not to tell Mr. Brenkman."

Copyright © BookheadEd Learning, LLC

148 Grinning with relief, we **simultaneously** clasped hands. "No matter what," Max reminded us.

149 To which I added, "Scout's Honor."

"Scout's Honor" by Avi. Copyright ©1996 by Avi. Originally appeared in WHEN I WAS YOUR AGE: Original Stories About Growing Up, published by Candlewick Press. Used by permission of Brandt & Hochman Literary Agents, Inc. All rights reserved.

Please note that excerpts and passages in the StudySync® library and this workbook are intended as touchstones to generate interest in an author's work. The excerpts and passages do not substitute for the reading of entire texts, and StudySync® strongly recommends that students seek out and purchase the whole literary or informational work in order to experience it as the author intended. Links to online resellers are available in our digital library. In addition, complete works may be ordered through an authorized reseller by filling out and returning to StudySync® the order form enclosed in this workbook.

Reading & Writing Companion 59

First Read

Read "Scout's Honor." After you read, complete the Think Questions below.

☁ THINK QUESTIONS

1. Where did the narrator grow up? How does that influence his idea of the "country"? Cite textual evidence from the selection to support your answer.

2. What happens to Max on the subway? What does the event reveal about their friendship?

3. How do Max and Horse react when the narrator suggests they head back home? Why does this surprise the narrator? Cite textual evidence from the selection to support your answer.

4. Find the word **absorbed** in paragraph 60 of "Scout's Honor." Use context clues in the surrounding sentences, as well as the sentence in which it appears, to determine the word's meaning. Write your definition here and identify clues that helped you figure out its meaning.

5. Use context clues to determine the meaning of **simultaneously** as it is used in paragraph 148 of "Scout's Honor." Write your definition here and identify clues that helped you figure out its meaning. Then check the meaning in a dictionary.

Skill:
Story Structure

Use the Checklist to analyze Story Structure in "Scout's Honor." Refer to the sample student annotations about Story Structure in the text.

In order to identify how a particular sentence, chapter, or scene fits into the overall structure of a text, note the following:

✓ the author's use of description, dialogue, and narration and how each develops the events of the plot

✓ the pattern the author uses to organize the events within a story or chapter

  • chronological, or in time order

  • events out of time order

✓ any literary devices the author uses, such as flashback, a part of a story that shows something that happened in the past

✓ any particular sentence, chapter, or scene that contributes to the development of the setting, the plot, and the theme

✓ how a particular sentence, chapter, or scene fits into the overall structure

To analyze how a particular sentence, chapter, or scene fits into the overall structure of a text and contributes to the development of the theme, setting, or plot, consider the following questions:

✓ What are the key events in the story and when did they take place?

✓ What impact does the order of events that take place in the story have on the theme, setting, or plot?

✓ What literary devices does the author use? How do they affect the development of the plot?

✓ How does a particular sentence, chapter, or scene fit into the overall structure? How does it contribute to the development of the theme, setting, or plot?

Skill:
Story Structure

Reread paragraphs 80–98 of "Scout's Honor." Then, using the Checklist on the previous page, answer the multiple-choice questions below.

⟳ YOUR TURN

1. Reread paragraph 81. Based on this paragraph, what can the reader conclude about the narrator?

   ○ A. The narrator is irritated with Horse because he does not know how to proceed bravely in this situation.

   ○ B. Although he attempts to be brave, the narrator is still feeling anxious about the journey to the country.

   ○ C. The narrator understands that Horse is unable to stay calm and tries to comfort him in his time of need.

   ○ D. Horse's anxiety creates a sense of tension between the boys, thus the narrator is unsettled.

2. Which of the following best describes the theme based on the passage provided?

   ○ A. Desperate times call for desperate measures.

   ○ B. In dark times, friends can offer the best support.

   ○ C. Blindly following others can cause trouble.

   ○ D. In life, we sometimes take on more than we can handle.

3. How does this passage contribute to the rest of the story's plot?

   ○ A. The events in the passage highlight the turning point of the plot because the boys are afraid.

   ○ B. The dialogue in the passage conveys a sense of urgency because the boys are not sure they will survive.

   ○ C. The passage emphasizes key, humbling events in the story that support the overall theme.

   ○ D. The narration in the passage highlights a dark tone that is maintained throughout the plot.

PLOT

sync skills

Skill:
Plot

Use the Checklist to analyze Plot in "Scout's Honor." Refer to the sample student annotations about Plot in the text.

In order to determine the plot and how a particular story's or drama's plot unfolds, note the following:

✓ specific plot events as they occur in the story

✓ the series of episodes as they occur

✓ ways characters respond or change as the plot moves toward a resolution

✓ dialogue between or among characters or actions that reveal their growth or change

To describe how a particular story's or drama's plot unfolds in a series of episodes as well as how the characters respond or change as the plot moves toward a resolution, consider the following questions:

✓ What is the plot? What are the key events in the plot?

✓ How does the series of episodes in the story help the plot unfold?

✓ How do the characters respond or change as the plot moves through the conflict and toward a resolution?

Please note that excerpts and passages in the StudySync® library and this workbook are intended as touchstones to generate interest in an author's work. The excerpts and passages do not substitute for the reading of entire texts, and StudySync® strongly recommends that students seek out and purchase the whole literary or informational work in order to experience it as the author intended. Links to online resellers are available in our digital library. In addition, complete works may be ordered through an authorized reseller by filling out and returning to StudySync® the order form enclosed in this workbook.

Reading & Writing
Companion

63

PLOT

Skill:
Plot

Reread paragraphs 129–139 from the text. Then, using the Checklist on the previous page, answer the multiple-choice questions below.

♻ YOUR TURN

1. Based on the narrator's thoughts in paragraph 129, the reader can conclude that —

   ○ A. the narrator's friends are close to giving up.
   ○ B. the narrator still doesn't think he's tough enough.
   ○ C. the boys are out of food.
   ○ D. the narrator is going to tell his friends that he gives up and wants to go home.

2. The turning point of the story is when —

   ○ A. Max shouts "food fight!"
   ○ B. the lean-to is knocked down.
   ○ C. the can of beans explodes all over them.
   ○ D. the boys eat the dirty franks.

3. Which paragraph includes the resolution of the story's conflict?

   ○ A. 138
   ○ B. 136
   ○ C. 139
   ○ D. 135

SCOUT'S HONOR

Close Read

Reread "Scout's Honor." As you reread, complete the Skills Focus questions below. Then use your answers and annotations from the questions to help you complete the Write activity.

◎ SKILLS FOCUS

1. Think about how the narrator reacts to the challenges the characters face. Identify what these reactions tell you about his personality.

2. Think about the beginning of the "Scout's Honor" when the narrator tells his friends he's going camping. Using textual evidence, explain why this scene is important to the rest of the story.

3. How boys can prove they are tough: this is the central conflict of Avi's story. Identify how each character reacts to key events in the plot as the boys try to resolve the conflict through their camping trip.

4. Use key events, including the inciting incident and moments of conflict, to determine how the resolution of the conflict contributes to the meaning of the story.

5. Identify how the development of the characters and plot in "Scout's Honor" connects to the Essential Question: "What do we do when life gets hard?"

✏ WRITE

LITERARY ANALYSIS: There are many challenges in "Scout's Honor" that the boys face. How do the characters' responses to these challenges help develop the plot and help readers interpret the events in the plot—such as the inciting incident, conflict, turning point and resolution—as they take place? Support your writing with evidence from the text.

The Good Samaritan

FICTION

René Saldaña, Jr.

2007

Introduction

René Saldaña, Jr.'s 2003 collection of short stories, *Finding Our Way*, features adolescents and young adults searching for answers wherever they are to be found. Encompassing universal experiences and rites of passage, Saldaña, Jr.'s stories take place in Hispanic neighborhoods ranging from Georgia to the south of Texas, where the author was born and raised. The collection's opening story, "The Good Samaritan," is told through the eyes of teenage Rey. As Rey's relationship with a neighborhood family turns sour, he soon finds himself faced with an age-old

"Let him do his own dirty work for once. He could stay out there and melt in this heat for all I cared."

1   I know he's in there, I thought. I saw the curtains of his bedroom move, only a little, yes, but they moved.

2   Yesterday Orlie told me, "Come over tomorrow afternoon. We'll hang out by the pool."

3   I rang the doorbell again. Then I knocked.

4   The door creaked open. The afternoon light crept into the dark living room inch by slow inch. Mrs. Sánchez, Orlie's mom, stuck her head through the narrow opening, her body hidden behind the door. "Hi, Rey, how can I help you?"

5   "Ah, Mrs. Sánchez, is Orlando here?" I tried looking past her but only saw a few pictures hanging on the wall. One of the Sánchez family all dressed up fancy and smiling, standing in front of a gray marble background.

6   "No, he's not. He went with his father to Mission."

7   "Oh, because Orlando said he would be here, and told me to come over."

8   "They won't be back until later tonight," she said. "You can come by tomorrow and see if he's here. You know how it is in the summer. He and his dad are always doing work here and there. Come back tomorrow, but call first."

9   "It's just that he said I could come by and swim in your pool. Dijo, 'Tomorrow, come over. I'll be here. We'll go swimming.'"

10 "I'm sorry he told you that, but without him or my husband here, you won't be able to use the pool," me dijo Mrs. Sánchez.

11 "Okay," I said.

12 "Maybe tomorrow?"

13 "Yeah, maybe."

14 But there was no maybe about it. I wouldn't be coming back. Because I knew that Orlando was in the house, he just didn't want to hang out. Bien codo con

su pool. Plain stingy. And tricky. This guy invited me and a few others over all summer to help his dad with some yard work because Mr. Sánchez told us, "If you help clean up the yard, you boys can use the pool any time you want so long as one of us is here." And we cleaned up his yard. On that hot day the water that smelled of chlorine looked delicious to me. And after a hard day's work cleaning his yard, I so looked forward to taking a dip. I'd even worn my trunks under my work clothes. Then Mr. Sánchez said, "Come by tomorrow. I don't want you fellas to track all this dirt into the pool."

15 "We can go home and shower and be back," said Hernando.

16 "No, mejor que regresen mañana. I'll be here tomorrow and we can swim. After lunch, okay. For sure we'll do it tomorrow," said Mr. Sánchez.

17 The following day he was there, but he was headed out right after lunch and he didn't feel safe leaving us behind without **supervision.** "If one of you drowns, your parents will be angry at me and…" He didn't say it, but he didn't need to. One of our parents could sue him. And he needed that like I needed another F in my Geometry I class!

18 Or, we figured out later, he could have just said, "I used you saps to do my dirty work. And I lied about the pool, suckers!"

19 I don't know why we hadn't learned our lesson. Twice before he had **hustled** us this way of our time and effort. Always dangling the carrot in front of our eyes, then snatching it away last second.

20 One of those times he promised us soft drinks and snacks if we helped clean up a yard across the street from his house. It wasn't his yard to worry about, but I guess he just didn't like to see the weeds growing as tall as dogs. What if he had company? What would they think? And he was angling for a position on the school board. How could a politico live in such filth!

21 Well, we did get a soft drink and chips, only it was one two-liter bottle of Coke and one bag of chips for close to ten of us. We had no cups, and the older, stronger boys got dibs on most of the eats. "I didn't know there'd be so many of you," he said. "Well, share. And thanks. You all are good, strong boys."

22 The next time was real hard **labor.** He said, "Help me dig these holes here, then we can put up some basketball rims. Once the cement dries on the court itself, you all can come over and play anytime since it's kind of your court too. That is, if you help me dig the holes."

23 And we did. We dug and dug and dug for close to six hours straight until we got done, passing on the shovel from one of us to the next. But we got it done. We had our court. Mr. Sánchez kept his word. He reminded us we could come over to play anytime, and we took special care not to dunk and grab hold of the rim. Even the shortest kid could practically dunk it because

Copyright © BookheadEd Learning, LLC

Skill: Summarizing

Rey recalls that he and his friends have been taken advantage of by Mr. Sánchez in the past.

The setting is a yard opposite Mr. Sánchez's house. It is so untidy and overgrown that Mr. Sánchez is afraid it will shame him in front of his guests.

Rey explains that he and his friends were promised a reward for their efforts, but the reward was smaller than Mr. Sánchez promised. They had to share a snack meant for a few people between the ten of them.

NOTES

the baskets were so low. But we'd seen the rims all bent down at the different yards at school. And we didn't want that for our court.

24 One day, we wanted to play a little three on three. After knocking on the different doors several times and getting no answer, we figured the Sánchez family had gone out. We decided that it'd be okay to play. We weren't going to do anything wrong. The court was far enough from the house that we couldn't possibly break a window. And Mr. Sánchez had said we could come over any time we wanted. It was our court, after all. Those were his words exactly.

25 A little later in the afternoon, Mr. Sánchez drove up in his truck, honking and honking at us. "Here they come. Maybe Orlando and Marty can play with us," someone said.

26 Pues, it was not to be. The truck had just come to a standstill when Mr. Sánchez shot out of the driver's side. He ran up to us, waving his hands in the air like a crazy man, first saying, then screaming, "What are you guys doing here? You all can't be here when I'm not here."

27 "But you told us we could come over anytime. And we knocked and knocked, and we were being very careful.'

28 "It doesn't matter. You all shouldn't be here when I'm not home. What if you had broken something?" he said.

29 "But we didn't," I said.

30 "But if you had, then who would have been responsible for paying to replace it? I'm sure every one of you would have denied breaking anything."

31 "Este vato!" said Hernando.

32 "Vato? Is that what you called me? I'm no street punk, no hoodlum. I'll have you know, I've worked my whole life, and I won't be called a vato. It's Mr. Sánchez. Got that? And you boys know what—from now on, you are not allowed to come here whether I'm home or not! You all messed it up for yourselves. You've shown me so much disrespect today you don't deserve to play on my court. It was a **privilege** and not a right, and you messed it up. Now leave!"

33 Hernando, who was fuming, said, "Orale, guys, let's go." He took the ball from one of the smaller boys and began to run toward the nearest basket. He slowed down the closer he came to the basket and leapt in the air. I'd never seen him jump with such grace. He floated from the foul line, his long hair like wings, all the way to the basket. He grabbed the ball in both his hands and let go of it at the last moment. Instead of dunking the ball, he let it shoot up to the sky; then he wrapped his fingers around the rim and pulled down as hard as

Skill:
Summarizing

Mr. Sánchez angrily kicks the boys off the basketball court. He feels disrespected. Mr. Sánchez says the boys were wrong to let themselves onto his property when he wasn't home.

he could, hanging on for a few seconds. Then the rest of us walked after him, dejected. He hadn't bent the rim even a millimeter. Eventually Orlie talked us into going back when his dad wasn't home. His baby brother, Marty, was small and slow, and Orlie wanted some competition on the court.

34   Today was it for me, though. I made up my mind never to go back to the Sánchezes'. I walked to the little store for a Fanta Orange. That and a grape Popsicle would cool me down. I sat on the bench outside, finished off the drink, returned the bottle for my nickel refund, and headed for home.

35   As soon as I walked through our front door, my mother said, "Mi'jo, you need to go pick up your brother at summer school. He missed the bus."

36   "Again? He probably missed it on purpose, Ama. He's always walking over to Leo's Grocery to talk to his little girlfriends, then he calls when he needs a ride." I turned toward the bedroom.

37   "Come back here," she said. So I turned and took a seat at the table. "Have you forgotten the times we had to go pick you up? Your brother always went with us, no matter what time it was."

38   "Yeah, but I was doing school stuff. Football, band. He's in summer school just piddling his time away!"

39   She looked at me as she brushed sweat away from her face with the back of her hand and said, "Just go pick him up, and hurry home. On the way back, stop at Circle Seven and buy some tortillas. There's money on the table."

40   I shook my head in disgust. Here I was, already a senior, having to be my baby brother's chauffeur.

41   I'd driven halfway to Leo's Grocery when I saw Mr. Sánchez's truck up ahead by the side of the road. I could just make him out sitting under the shade of his truck. Every time he heard a car coming his way, he'd raise his head slightly, try to catch the driver's attention by staring at him, then he'd hang his head again when the car didn't stop.

42   I slowed down as I **approached.** Could he tell it was me driving? When he looked up at my car, I could swear he almost smiled, thinking he had been saved. He had been leaning his head between his bent knees, and I could tell he was tired; his white shirt stuck to him because of all the sweat. His sock on one leg was bunched up at his ankle like a carnation. He had the whitest legs I'd ever seen on a Mexican. Whiter than even my dad's. I kept on looking straight; that is, I made like I was looking ahead, not a care in the world, but out of the corner of my eye I saw that he had a flat tire, that he had gotten two of the lug nuts off but hadn't gotten to the others, that the crowbar lay half on his other foot and half on the ground beside him, that his hair was matted by sweat to his forehead.

43   I knew that look. I'd probably looked just like that digging those holes for our basketball court, cleaning up his yard and the one across the street from his house. I wondered if he could use a cold two-liter Coke right about now! If he was dreaming of taking a dip in his pool!

44   I drove on. No way was I going to help him out again! Let him do his own dirty work for once. He could stay out there and melt in this heat for all I cared. And besides, someone else will stop, I thought. Someone who doesn't know him like I do.

45   And I knew that when Mr. Sánchez got home, he'd stop at my house on his walk around the barrio. My dad would be watering the plants, his evening ritual to relax from a hard day at work, and Mr. Sánchez would mention in passing that I had probably not seen him by the side of the road so I hadn't stopped to help him out; "Kids today" he would say to my dad, "not a care in the world, their heads up in the clouds somewhere." My dad would call me out and ask me to tell him and Mr. Sánchez why I hadn't helped out a neighbor when he needed it most. I'd say, to both of them, "That was you? I thought you and Orlie were in Mission taking care of some business, so it never **occurred** to me to stop to help a neighbor. Geez, I'm so sorry." Or I could say, "You know, I was in such a hurry to pick up my brother in La Joya that I didn't even notice you by the side of the road."

46   I'd be off the hook. Anyways, why should I be the one to extend a helping hand when he's done every one of us in the barrio wrong in one way or another! He deserves to sweat a little. A taste of his own bad medicine. Maybe he'll learn a lesson.

47   But I remembered the look in his eyes as I drove past him. That same tired look my father had when he'd get home from work and he didn't have the strength to take off his boots. My father always looked like he'd been working for centuries without any rest. He'd sit there in front of the television on his favorite green vinyl sofa chair and stare at whatever was on TV. He'd sit there for an hour before he could move, before he could eat his supper and take his shower, that same look on his face Mr. Sánchez had just now.

48   What if this were my dad stranded on the side of the road? I'd want someone to stop for him.

49   "My one good deed for today," I told myself. "And I'm doing it for my dad really, not for Mr. Sánchez."

50   I made a U-turn, drove back to where he was still sitting, turned around again, and pulled up behind him.

51   "I thought that was you, Rey," he said. He wiped at his forehead with his shirtsleeve. "And when you drove past, I thought you hadn't seen me. Thank

Please note that excerpts and passages in the StudySync® library and this workbook are intended as touchstones to generate interest in an author's work. The excerpts and passages do not substitute for the reading of entire texts, and StudySync® strongly recommends that students seek out and purchase the whole literary or informational work in order to experience it as the author intended. Links to online resellers are available in our digital library. In addition, complete works may be ordered through an authorized reseller by filling out and returning to StudySync® the order form enclosed in this workbook.

Reading & Writing
Companion

71

goodness you stopped. I've been here for close to forty-five minutes and nobody's stopped to help. Thank goodness you did. I just can't get the tire off."

52   Thank my father, I thought. If it weren't for my father, you'd still be out here.

53   I had that tire changed in no time. All the while Mr. Sánchez stood behind me and a bit to my left saying, "Yes, thank God you came by. Boy, it's hot out here. You're a good boy, Rey. You'll make a good man. How about some help there?"

54   "No, I've got it," I answered. "I'm almost done."

55   "Oyes, Rey, what if you come over tomorrow night to my house? I'm having a little barbecue for some important people here in town. You should come over. We're even going to do some swimming. What do you say?"

56   I tightened the last of the nuts, replaced the jack, the flat tire, and the crowbar in the bed of his truck, looked at him, and said, "Thanks. But I'll be playing football with the vatos."

First Read

Read "The Good Samaritan." After you read, complete the Think Questions below.

☁ **THINK QUESTIONS**

1. Why is Rey upset with Orlie at the beginning of the story? Cite textual evidence from the selection to support your answer.

2. Why does Rey hold a grudge against Mr. Sánchez? Cite textual evidence from the selection to support your answer.

3. What is the main problem Rey faces at the end of the story? What actions does he take? Cite textual evidence from the selection to support your answer.

4. Find the word **labor** in paragraph 22 of "The Good Samaritan." Use context clues in the surrounding sentences, as well as the sentence in which the word appears, to determine the word's meaning. Write your definition here and identify clues that helped you figure out its meaning.

5. Use context clues to determine the meaning of **approached** as it is used in paragraph 42 of "The Good Samaritan." Write your definition here and identify clues that helped you figure out its meaning. Then check the meaning in a dictionary.

Please note that excerpts and passages in the StudySync® library and this workbook are intended as touchstones to generate interest in an author's work. The excerpts and passages do not substitute for the reading of entire texts, and StudySync® strongly recommends that students seek out and purchase the whole literary or informational work in order to experience it as the author intended. Links to online resellers are available in our digital library. In addition, complete works may be ordered through an authorized reseller by filling out and returning to StudySync® the order form enclosed in this workbook.

Reading & Writing Companion   **73**

Skill:
Summarizing

Use the Checklist to analyze Summarizing in "The Good Samaritan." Refer to the sample student annotations about Summarizing in the text.

••• CHECKLIST FOR SUMMARIZING

In order to determine how to write an objective summary of a text, note the following:

- ✓ in literature, note the setting, characters, and events in the plot, taking into account the main problem the characters face and how it is solved

- ✓ answers to the basic questions *who, what, where, when, why,* and *how*

- ✓ stay objective, and do not add your own personal thoughts, judgments, or opinions to the summary

To provide an objective summary of a text not influenced by personal opinions or judgments, consider the following questions:

- ✓ What are the answers to basic *who, what, where, when, why,* and *how* questions in literature?

- ✓ Are all of the details I have included in my summary of a work of literature important?

- ✓ Is my summary objective, or have I added my own thoughts, judgments, or personal opinions?

Skill:
Summarizing

Reread paragraphs 42–44 of "The Good Samaritan." Then, using the Checklist on the previous page, answer the multiple-choice questions below.

🔁 YOUR TURN

1. Which of the following best describes Rey's relationship with Mr. Sánchez in this selection?

   ○ A. Mr. Sánchez is like a father figure to Rey.
   ○ B. Rey thinks that Mr. Sánchez treats him unfairly.
   ○ C. Mr. Sánchez relies on Rey to do things that he cannot.
   ○ D. Rey pities Mr. Sánchez as he wishes he could help.

2. Which of the following answer choices provides the best summary of this selection?

   ○ A. Rey recalls times when Mr. Sánchez has used him and does not want to help him fix the flat tire.
   ○ B. Mr. Sánchez gets a flat tire and wishes he hadn't taken advantage of Rey in the past.
   ○ C. Rey sees Mr. Sánchez struggling to fix a flat tire and decides to help him out.
   ○ D. Mr. Sánchez observes Rey passing him up in his time of need.

Close Read

Reread "The Good Samaritan." As you reread, complete the Skills Focus questions below. Then use your answers and annotations from the questions to help you complete the Write activity.

◎ SKILLS FOCUS

1. Summarize the lessons Rey learns as he deals with the Sánchez family without giving your personal opinion.

2. Think about how Rey makes decisions in "The Good Samaritan." Use evidence of Rey's decision-making to explain his character.

3. Use textual evidence to explain why making the decision to help Mr. Sánchez was hard for Rey.

✏ WRITE

DEBATE: Rey lives up to the story's title, "The Good Samaritan," when he stops to help Mr. Sánchez. However, do you think Rey made the right decision in stopping to help? Summarize Rey's experiences dealing with the Sánchez family and use them to prepare an argument for a debate. Use evidence from the text to support your position.

Jabberwocky

POETRY
Lewis Carroll
1872

Introduction

studysync TV

This whimsical poem about a heroic quest was first published in its entirety in author Lewis Carroll's *Through the Looking Glass*. Carroll (1832–1898) is best known for his fanciful stories and his contributions to the genre of literary nonsense. His most famous work, *Alice's Adventures in Wonderland*, has been adapted for film and television, and continues to be well-beloved today. In its sequel, *Through the Looking Glass*, Alice finds "Jabberwocky" in a curious book after she steps through a mirror into an odd new world. The poem's fantastical characters, invented language, and formal structure have made it a classic in its own right.

"'Beware the Jabberwock, my son! The jaws that bite, the claws that catch! . . .'"

from Chapter 1: "Looking-Glass House"

1   'Twas brillig, and the slithy toves
2   Did gyre and gimble in the wabe;
3   All mimsy were the borogoves,
4   And the mome raths outgrabe.

5   'Beware the Jabberwock, my son!
6   The jaws that bite, the claws that catch!
7   Beware the Jubjub bird, and **shun**
8   The frumious Bandersnatch!'

9   He took his vorpal sword in hand:
10 Long time the manxome **foe** he **sought**—
11 So rested he by the Tumtum tree
12 And stood awhile in thought.

13 And, as in uffish thought he stood,
14 The Jabberwock, with eyes of flame,
15 Came whiffling through the tulgey wood,
16 And burbled as it came!

17 One, two! One, two! And through and through
18 The vorpal blade went snicker-snack!
19 He left it dead, and with its head
20 He went **galumphing** back.

21 'And hast thou slain the Jabberwock?
22 Come to my arms, my beamish boy!
23 O frabjous day! Callooh! Callay!'
24 He **chortled** in his joy.

25 'Twas brillig, and the slithy toves
26 Did gyre and gimble in the wabe;
27 All mimsy were the borogoves,
28 And the mome raths outgrabe.

The Jabberwock

Copyright © BookheadEd Learning, LLC

WRITE

POETRY: The poem "Jabberwocky" uses nonsense language to describe a heroic battle. Choose two nonsensical words from the first stanza of "Jabberwocky" and create a definition for each based on context, sound, and the image you picture in your head. Then write a poem about a time you overcame an obstacle incorporating each of the two words.

Please note that excerpts and passages in the StudySync® library and this workbook are intended as touchstones to generate interest in an author's work. The excerpts and passages do not substitute for the reading of entire texts, and StudySync® strongly recommends that students seek out and purchase the whole literary or informational work in order to experience it as the author intended. Links to online resellers are available in our digital library. In addition, complete works may be ordered through an authorized reseller by filling out and returning to StudySync® the order form enclosed in this workbook.

Reading & Writing Companion 79

Gathering Blue

FICTION
Lois Lowry
2000

Introduction

Lois Lowry (b. 1937) has written more than 30 novels for children and young adults in her long career. The novel excerpted here, *Gathering Blue*, takes place in the same universe as several other novels of Lowry's, including 1993's Newbery-winning *The Giver*. Prior to this excerpt from Chapter 5, a young girl, Kira, has been left an orphan after her mother's death. Having been born with a twisted leg in a place where the weak and disabled are typically left in the fields to die, Kira fears she will be forced to leave—unless her talent for embroidery can earn her a role in society. She awaits judgment from Jamison and the Council of Guardians over a dispute between her and Vandara, an enemy of hers who seeks her expulsion.

"The proceedings are complete. We have reached our decision."

from Chapter 5

1   Kira noticed for the first time that a large box had been placed on the floor behind the seats of the Council of Guardians.

2   It had not been there before the lunchtime break.

3   As she and Vandara watched, one of the guards, responding to a nod from the chief guardian, lifted the box to the table and raised its lid. Her defender, Jamison, removed and unfolded something that she recognized immediately.

4   "The Singer's robe!" Kira spoke aloud in delight.

5   "This has no **relevance,**" Vandara muttered. But she too was leaning forward to see.

6   The magnificent robe was laid out on the table in display. Ordinarily it was seen only once a year, at the time when the village gathered to hear the Ruin Song, the lengthy history of their people. Most citizens, crowded into the auditorium for the occasion, saw the Singer's robe only from a distance; they shoved and pushed, trying to nudge closer for a look.

7   But Kira knew the robe well from watching her mother's meticulous work on it each year. A guardian had always stood nearby, attentive. Warned not to touch, Kira had watched, marveling at her mother's skill, at her ability to choose just the right shade.

8   There, on the left shoulder! Kira remembered that spot, where just last year some threads had pulled and torn and her mother had carefully coaxed the broken threads free. Then she had selected pale pinks, slightly darker roses, and other colors darkening to crimson, each hue only a hint deeper than the one before; and she had stitched them into place, blending them flawlessly into the edges of the **elaborate** design.

9   Jamison watched Kira as she remembered. Then he said, "Your mother had been teaching you the art."

10 Kira nodded. "Since I was small," she acknowledged aloud.

11 "Your mother was a skilled worker. Her dyes were **steadfast.** They have not faded."

12 "She was careful," Kira said, "and thorough."

13 "We are told that your skill is greater than hers."

14 *So they knew.* "I still have much to learn," Kira said.

15 "And she taught you the coloring, as well as the stitches?"

16 Kira nodded because she knew he expected her to. But it was not exactly true. Her mother had planned to teach her the art of the dyes, but the time had not yet come before the illness struck. She tried to be honest in her answer. "She was beginning to teach me," Kira said. "She told me that she had been taught by a woman named Annabel."

17 "Annabella now," Jamison said.

18 Kira was startled. "She is still alive? And four syllables?"

19 "She is very old. Her sight is somewhat **diminished.** But she can still be used as a **resource.**"

20 *Resource for what?* But Kira stayed silent. The scrap in her pocket was warm against her hand.

21 Suddenly Vandara stood. "I request that these proceedings continue," she said abruptly and harshly. "This is a delaying tactic on the part of the defender."

22 The chief guardian rose. Around him, the other guardians, who had been murmuring among themselves, fell silent.

23 His voice, directed at Vandara, was not unkind. "You may go," he said. "The proceedings are complete. We have reached our decision."

24 Vandara stood silent, unmoving. She glared at him defiantly. The chief guardian nodded, and two guards moved forward to escort her from the room.

25 "I have a right to know your decision!" Vandara shouted, her face twisted with rage. She wrested her arms free of the guards' grasp and faced the Council of Guardians.

26 "Actually," the chief guardian said in a calm voice, "you have no rights at all. But I am going to tell you the decision so that there will be no misunderstanding.

27 "The orphan girl Kira will stay. She will have a new role."

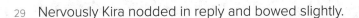

28 He gestured toward the Singer's robe, still spread out on the table. "Kira," he said, looking at her, "you will continue your mother's work. You will go beyond her work, actually, since your skill is far greater than hers was. First, you will repair the robe, as your mother always did. Next, you will restore it. Then your true work will begin. You will *complete* the robe." He gestured toward the large undecorated expanse of fabric across the shoulders. He raised one eyebrow, looking at her as if he were asking a question.

29 Nervously Kira nodded in reply and bowed slightly.

30 "As for you?" The chief guardian looked again at Vandara, who stood sullenly between the guards. He spoke politely to her. "You have not lost. You demanded the girl's land, and you may have it, you and the other women. Build your pen. It would be wise to pen your tykes; they are troublesome and should be better contained.

31 "Go now," he commanded.

32 Vandara turned. Her face was a mask of fury. She shrugged away the hands of the guards, leaned forward, and whispered harshly to Kira, "You will fail. Then they will kill you."

33 She smiled coldly at Jamison. "So, that's it, then," she said. "The girl is yours." She stalked down the aisle and went through the broad door.

34 The chief guardian and the other Council members ignored the outburst, as if it were merely an annoying insect that had finally been swatted away. Someone was refolding the Singer's robe.

35 "Kira," Jamison said, "go and gather what you need. Whatever you want to bring with you. Be back here when the bell rings four times. And we will take you to your quarters, to the place where you will live from now on."

36 Puzzled, Kira waited a moment. But there were no other instructions. The guardians were straightening their papers and collecting their books and belongings. They seemed to have forgotten she was there. Finally she stood, straightened herself against her walking stick, and limped from the room.

37 Emerging from the Council Edifice into bright sunlight and the usual chaos of the village central plaza, she realized that it was still midafternoon, still an ordinary day in the existence of the people, and that no one's life had changed except her own.

Excerpted from *Gathering Blue* by Lois Lowry, published by Ember.

WRITE

PERSONAL RESPONSE: Think back to a challenge that you've faced in your life. How did you feel facing it? How were you able to respond? With that memory in mind, what advice would you give Kira from *Gathering Blue* to help her with the challenge she faces now?

A Wrinkle in Time

FICTION
Madeleine L'Engle
1962

Introduction

studysync tv

eg Murry and her precocious younger brother, Charles Wallace, will do anything they can to find their father. Did their father's top-secret experiments with time-travel cause his mysterious disappearance? What evil forces are holding him hostage? In *A Wrinkle in Time* by Madeleine L'Engle (1918–2007), Meg and Charles embark on a dangerous journey to find the answers, joined by their young neighbor, Calvin. In the excerpt, they have arrived on distant planet Camazotz, where they encounter a strange man with a fixed, red-eyed gaze. Telepathically, he urges them to merge their thoughts with his. First published in 1963, L'Engle's beloved novel won a Newbery Medal, the Sequoyah Book Award, and the Lewis Carroll Shelf

"The only reason we are here is because we think our father is here. Can you tell us where to find him?"

NOTES

from Chapter 7: The Man with Red Eyes

1   "Once ten is ten. Once eleven is eleven. Once twelve is twelve."

2   The number words pounded insistently against Meg's brain. They seemed to be boring their way into her skull.

3   "Twice one is two. Twice two is four. Twice three is six."

4   Calvin's voice came out in an angry shout. "Fourscore and seven years ago our fathers brought forth on this continent a new nation, **conceived** in liberty, and dedicated to the proposition that all men are created equal."

5   "Twice four is eight. Twice five is ten. Twice six is twelve."

6   "Father!" Meg screamed. "Father!" The scream, half involuntary, jerked her mind back out of darkness.

7   The words of the multiplication table seemed to break up into laughter. "Splendid! Splendid! You have passed your **preliminary** tests with flying colors."

8   "You didn't think we were as easy as all that, falling for that old stuff, did you?" Charles Wallace demanded.

9   "Ah, I hoped not. I most sincerely hoped not. But after all you are very young and very impressionable, and the younger the better, my little man. The younger the better."

10 Meg looked up at the fiery eyes, at the light pulsing above them, and then away. She tried looking at the mouth, at the thin, almost colorless lips, and this was more possible, even though she had to look obliquely, so that she was not sure exactly what the face really looked like, whether it was young or old, cruel or kind, human or alien.

11 "If you please," she said, trying to sound calm and brave. "The only reason we are here is because we think our father is here. Can you tell us where to find him?"

Skill:
Context Clues

Meg seems to be having a hard time looking directly at the man. The words "not sure exactly what the face really looked like" suggest that she is looking at him sideways, or indirectly. So obliquely must mean "indirectly." Meg can't tell whether he is young or old or if he's even human!

12   "Ah, your father!" There seemed to be a great chortling of delight. "Ah, yes, your father! It is not *can* I, you know, young lady, but *will* I?"

13   "Will you, then?"

14   "That depends on a number of things. Why do you want your father?"

15   "Didn't you ever have a father yourself?" Meg demanded. "You don't want him for a *reason*. You want him because he's your *father*."

16   "Ah, but he hasn't been *acting* very like a father, lately, has he? **Abandoning** his wife and his four little children to go gallivanting off on wild adventures of his own."

17   "He was working for the government. He'd never have left us otherwise. And we want to see him, please. Right now."

18   "My, but the little miss is impatient! Patience, patience, young lady."

19   Meg did not tell the man on the chair that patience was not one of her virtues.

20   "And by the way, my children," he continued blandly, "you don't need to vocalize verbally with me, you know. I can understand you quite as well as you can understand me."

21   Charles Wallace put his hands on his hips defiantly. "The spoken word is one of the triumphs of man," he proclaimed, "and I intend to continue using it, particularly with people I don't trust." But his voice was shaking. Charles Wallace, who even as an infant had seldom cried, was near tears.

22   "And you don't trust me?"

23   "What reason have you given us to trust you?"

24   "What cause have I given you for distrust?" The thin lips curled slightly.

25   Suddenly Charles Wallace darted forward and hit the man as hard as he could, which was fairly hard, as he had had a good deal of coaching from the twins.

26   "Charles!" Meg screamed.

27   The men in dark smocks moved smoothly but with swiftness to Charles. The man in the chair casually raised one finger, and the men dropped back.

28   "Hold it—" Calvin whispered, and together he and Meg darted forward and grabbed Charles Wallace, pulling him back from the platform.

29   The man gave a wince and the thought of his voice was a little breathless, as though Charles Wallace's punch had succeeded in winding him. "May I ask why you did that?"

30 "Because you aren't you," Charles Wallace said. "I'm not sure what you are, but you"—he pointed to the man on the chair—"aren't what's talking to us. I'm sorry if I hurt you. I didn't think you were real. I thought perhaps you were a robot, because I don't feel anything coming directly from you. I'm not sure where it's coming from, but it's coming through you. It isn't you."

31 "Pretty smart, aren't you?" the thought asked, and Meg had an uncomfortable feeling that she detected a snarl.

32 "It's not that I'm smart," Charles Wallace said, and again Meg could feel the palm of his hand sweating inside hers.

33 "Try to find out who I am, then," the thought probed.

34 "I have been trying," Charles Wallace said, his voice high and troubled.

35 "Look into my eyes. Look deep within them and I will tell you."

36 Charles Wallace looked quickly at Meg and Calvin, then said, as though to himself, "I have to," and focused his clear blue eyes on the red ones of the man in the chair. Meg looked not at the man but at her brother. After a moment it seemed that his eyes were no longer focusing. The pupils grew smaller and smaller, as though he were looking into an **intensely** bright light, until they seemed to close entirely, until his eyes were nothing but an opaque blue. He slipped his hands out of Meg's and Calvin's and started walking slowly toward the man on the chair.

37 "No!" Meg screamed. "No!"

38 But Charles Wallace continued his slow walk forward, and she knew that he had not heard her.

39 "No!" she screamed again, and ran after him. With her inefficient flying tackle she landed on him. She was so much larger than he that he fell sprawling, hitting his head a sharp crack against the marble floor. She knelt by him, sobbing. After a moment of lying there as though he had been knocked out by the blow, he opened his eyes, shook his head, and sat up. Slowly the pupils of his eyes dilated until they were back to normal, and the blood came back to his white cheeks.

40 The man on the chair spoke directly into Meg's mind, and now there was a **distinct** menace to the words. "I am not pleased," he said to her. "I could very easily lose patience with you, and that, for your information, young lady, would not be good for your father. If you have the slightest desire to see your father again, you had better cooperate."

Excerpted from *A Wrinkle in Time* by Madeleine L'Engle, published by Farrar, Straus and Giroux.

First Read

Read *A Wrinkle in Time*. After you read, complete the Think Questions below.

1. The voice says that Meg, Calvin, and Charles have passed their "preliminary tests." What tests have they passed, and how? Cite textual evidence from the selection to support your answer.

2. Write two or three sentences contrasting Charles Wallace with Meg and Calvin.

3. The author alludes to the saying "Patience is a virtue." How does Meg demonstrate a lack of patience in the text? Cite textual evidence from the selection to support your answer.

4. Find the word **abandoning** in paragraph 16 of *A Wrinkle in Time*. Use context clues in the surrounding sentences, as well as the sentence in which the word appears, to determine the word's meaning. Write your definition here and identify clues that helped you figure out its meaning.

5. Use context clues to determine the meaning of **intensely** as it is used in paragraph 36 of *A Wrinkle in Time*. Write your definition here and identify clues that helped you figure out its meaning. Then check the meaning in the dictionary.

Please note that excerpts and passages in the StudySync® library and this workbook are intended as touchstones to generate interest in an author's work. The excerpts and passages do not substitute for the reading of entire texts, and StudySync® strongly recommends that students seek out and purchase the whole literary or informational work in order to experience it as the author intended. Links to online resellers are available in our digital library. In addition, complete works may be ordered through an authorized reseller by filling out and returning to StudySync® the order form enclosed in this workbook.

Reading & Writing Companion

89

Skill:
Context Clues

Use the Checklist to analyze Context Clues in *A Wrinkle in Time*. Refer to the sample student annotations about Context Clues in the text.

••• CHECKLIST FOR CONTEXT CLUES

In order to use context as a clue to infer the meaning of a word, note the following:

✓ clues about the word's part of speech

✓ clues in the surrounding text about the word's meaning

✓ signal words that cue a type of context clue, such as:

- *for example* or *for instance* to signal an example context clue
- *like, similarly,* or *just as* to signal a comparison clue
- *but, however,* or *unlike* to signal a contrast context clue

To determine the meaning of a word as it is used in a text, consider the following questions:

✓ What is the overall sentence, paragraph, or text about?

✓ How does the word function in the sentence?

✓ What clues can help me determine the word's part of speech?

✓ What textual clues can help me figure out the word's definition?

✓ Are there any examples that show what the word means?

✓ What do I think the word means?

To verify the preliminary determination of the meaning of the word based on context, consider the following questions:

✓ Does the definition I inferred make sense within the context of the sentence?

✓ Which of the dictionary's definitions makes sense within the context of the sentence?

Copyright © BookheadEd Learning, LLC

Skill:
Context Clues

Reread paragraphs 20–24 of *A Wrinkle in Time*. Then, using the Checklist on the previous page, answer the multiple-choice questions below.

↻ YOUR TURN

1. This question has two parts. First, answer Part A. Then answer Part B.

    Part A: Which of the following words or phrases most closely matches the definition of **defiantly** as it is used in the passage?

    ○ A. in a manner that shows open resistance
    ○ B. in a manner that shows fear
    ○ C. in a manner that shows sadness
    ○ D. in a manner that shows entertainment

    Part B: Which of the following words or phrases from the passage best supports the answer to Part A?

    ○ A. "triumph"
    ○ B. "voice was shaking"
    ○ C. "infant"
    ○ D. "put his hands on his hips"

Please note that excerpts and passages in the StudySync® library and this workbook are intended as touchstones to generate interest in an author's work. The excerpts and passages do not substitute for the reading of entire texts, and StudySync® strongly recommends that students seek out and purchase the whole literary or informational work in order to experience it as the author intended. Links to online resellers are available in our digital library. In addition, complete works may be ordered through an authorized reseller by filling out and returning to StudySync® the order form enclosed in this workbook.

Reading & Writing Companion   91

Close Read

Reread *A Wrinkle in Time*. As you reread, complete the Skills Focus questions below. Then use your answers and annotations from the questions to help you complete the Write activity.

◎ SKILLS FOCUS

1. Think about the word choices Madeleine L'Engle makes in *A Wrinkle in Time*. Identify examples of unknown words and what context clues you used to understand them.

2. Identify the words and phrases the author uses to describe the setting, and explain how you used context clues to understand them.

3. Using context clues, identify how the characters in *A Wrinkle in Time* feel and how you would feel if you were in their situation. Support your description with textual evidence.

4. In "Jabberwocky," Lewis Carroll uses nonsensical words. In *Gathering Blue*, Lois Lowry uses descriptive language. Identify passages in *A Wrinkle in Time* where L'Engle uses language in similar ways to Carroll's or Lowry's.

5. Meg, Calvin, and Charles Wallace are dealing with the challenge of understanding the unknown in *A Wrinkle in Time*. Explain how their experiences change their perspectives of the Man with Red Eyes. Support your explanation with textual evidence.

✏ WRITE

COMPARE AND CONTRAST: "Jabberwocky" and *A Wrinkle in Time* both have eerie language. *A Wrinkle in Time* and *Gathering Blue* both feature settings and events that make the reader feel uncertain. How does using context clues help you understand these unique selections? Compare the language and context clues you used in *A Wrinkle in Time* with those in one of the other two selections. Remember to support your ideas with evidence from the texts.

Extended
Writing
Project and
Grammar

EXTENDED
WRITING
PROJECT
NARRATIVE
WRITING

Narrative Writing Process: Plan

PLAN	DRAFT	REVISE	EDIT AND PUBLISH

The challenges that a character faces in a story are what make the story interesting. Sometimes a character is faced with a major challenge that is a matter of life and death, like Brian Robeson in *Hatchet*. At other times the challenge might be something small and seemingly insignificant, but it has a major effect on the character.

WRITING PROMPT

How can an unexpected event turn into a major challenge?

Imagine the very worst possible day. What event or individual makes that day so terrible? How do your characters respond? Write a story in which the main character faces an unexpected challenge on what was supposed to be a normal day. Regardless of the challenge you choose, be sure your narrative includes the following:

- a plot with a beginning, middle, and end
- a detailed setting
- characters and dialogue
- an interesting challenge
- a clear theme

Introduction to Narrative Writing

Narrative writing tells a story. It includes experiences or events that have been imagined by a writer. Good fiction writing uses effective techniques. These include relevant descriptive details and a structure with a series of events that contain a beginning, middle, and end. The characteristics of fiction writing include:

- setting
- characters
- plot
- theme
- point of view

As you continue with this Extended Writing Project, you'll receive more instruction and practice at crafting each of the characteristics of fiction writing to create your own narrative.

Before you get started on your own narrative, read this narrative that one student, Nik, wrote in response to the writing prompt. As you read the Model, highlight and annotate the features of narrative writing that Nik included in his narrative.

☰ STUDENT MODEL

An Unexpected Challenge

1   Even before he opened his eyes that Saturday morning, Tyler could hear the sirens. He tried to turn over and go back to sleep, but the piercing sound grew louder. Then he smelled smoke. Was his house on fire? Where were his parents? Tyler leaped out of bed and ran to the window. He gripped the windowsill tightly as he took in the scene. Smoke was pouring out of the house across the way. Three fire trucks, their lights blinking, were parked in the street. Mr. Molano stood on the curb in his pajamas, gesturing wildly.

2   Tyler flew to his bedroom door and flung it open. "Dad?!" he yelled, looking around wildly. "DAD!"

3   "Tyler? I could use your help down here!"

4   Tyler dashed down the stairs. His father was standing in the kitchen. He was holding the Molanos' infant daughter, Tonya. She was trying hard to keep her eyes open. Next to him, their 8-year-old son Max stood staring. He looked like he was in shock.

5   "I was just going to get you," Tyler's father said. "You saw the fire? Luckily no one has been seriously hurt. Look, I know this is a lot to ask, but I need your help here. Mrs. Molano has been taken to the hospital. I think she'll be fine, but Mr. Molano is too upset to drive. I have to take him to the hospital, and I need you to watch Tonya and Max until I get back."

6   Suddenly Tyler looked like *he* was in shock. "Look after *Tonya?* Dad, is she even a year old? I don't know how to. . ."

7   Tyler's father cut him off. "Tyler, I know this is a lot to ask. But your mom is at her office seeing patients until noon. There's no one else who can do this right now. Mr. Molano's sister is coming to see to their house, but she lives an hour away."

NOTES

8   "But . . ."

9   "Tonya will probably sleep until we get back, Tyler. I'll place her in your bed and surround her with pillows so she'll be safe. See if you can get Max to eat some breakfast. Then take him up to your room so you can watch Tonya."

10   Almost before Tyler knew it, his father had swept up the stairs and then out the door. Tyler just stood there. Slowly, he looked down at Max. "Um, would you like some breakfast, Max?" he said. The boy just nodded, and Tyler led him over to the kitchen table.

11   Tyler thought about making pancakes. He had watched his father make them often enough. But it would take too long. He opened a cabinet and pulled out some cereal.

12   "Is this okay, Max?" Tyler asked.

13   The boy nodded again. Then, unexpectedly, he burst into tears. "I want my mom!" he wailed.

14   Tyler froze. What should he do? Then he remembered what his father had said—Mrs. Molano would be all right.

15   Tyler patted the boy on the shoulder. As he poured some cereal into a bowl, he said, "Don't worry, buddy. Your mom will be okay. The doctors at the hospital will take good care of her. My dad said he thought she would be fine. You'll see."

16   Max looked up at Tyler. He sniffed a few times and then smiled weakly. Tyler went to get him some tissues so Max could wipe his eyes.

17   After Max finished his cereal, Tyler said, "Let's go check on Tonya. Also, I've got a big picture book about space pirates I think you're going to like!"

18   Max grinned and Tyler felt a flood of relief. He wasn't sure how he would deal with Max if he started crying again.

19   Soon Max was sitting on the floor reading. For a moment, everything was wonderfully quiet. Tyler walked over to the window and peered out. The fire seemed under control. There was no more smoke at least. Best of all, it didn't seem as if the house had been damaged very much.

20   Then, suddenly, Tonya woke up. It was as if someone had flipped a switch. The tiny baby went from a sound sleep to full-on crying mode. Tyler's eyes widened and he looked at Max. "What should I do?" he asked.

21   "Mom always picks her up," Max said.

22   Tyler bent over and carefully picked up the baby. He was terrified that he might drop her. But she still cried.

23   "Okay, now what?" Tyler asked.

24   "You should walk around with her."

25   Tyler walked around the bedroom and into the hallway with the baby. The motion seemed to calm her down. But anytime Tyler stopped walking, Tonya began crying again. "Okay, Tonya, you're the boss. I'll keep walking," Tyler said.

26   After Tyler had circled the hallway for what felt like the five-hundredth time, his mom came home. Tyler had never been so glad to see her in his life.

27   "Well, look at you!" Mom said. "You're an expert baby walker. May I hold her?"

28   "You bet. Boy, my arms are tired!"

29   As his mother scooped Tonya into her arms, she said, "Great job, Tyler. Dad called me from the hospital and told me what was going on. I got here as soon as I could, but it looks like you didn't even need my help. I'm really proud of you for rising to the challenge and helping out."

30   "Dad and Max were the real experts," Tyler said. "I just did what they told me to do."

31   Tyler's mother turned to smile at Max. "Your mom's going to be fine, Max," she said. "She'll be home tomorrow."

32   Max clapped and at the same time Tonya started crying again. Tyler's mother placed the baby back in Tyler's arms.

33   "Here," she laughed. "You're the champion baby walker!"

Copyright © BookheadEd Learning, LLC

✏ WRITE

Writers often take notes about story ideas before they sit down to write. Think about what you've learned so far about organizing narrative writing to help you begin prewriting.

- **Genre:** In what sort of genre would you like to write? Most any genre can include focus on an unexpected challenge. Genres include realistic fiction, science fiction, fantasy, or mystery, to name some examples.

- **Characters:** What kinds of characters will you include in your narrative?

- **Plot:** What would a normal day be like for your character or characters? What could happen that would pose a challenge for them?

- **Plot/Character:** How will your character or characters respond to the challenge?

- **Setting:** How might the setting of your story affect the characters and the challenges they face?

- **Point of View:** From which point of view should your story be told, and why?

Response Instructions

Use the questions in the bulleted list to write a one-paragraph summary. Your summary should describe what will happen in your narrative, like the one above.

Don't worry about including all of the details now; focus only on the most essential and important elements. You will refer back to this short summary as you continue through the steps of the writing process.

Copyright © BookheadEd Learning, LLC

Skill:
Organizing Narrative Writing

••• CHECKLIST FOR ORGANIZING NARRATIVE WRITING

As you consider how to organize your writing for your narrative, use the following questions as a guide:

- Who is the narrator and who are the characters in the story?

- Where will the story take place?

- What conflict or problem will the characters have to resolve?

- Have I created a series of plot events that flow logically and naturally from one event to the next?

Here are some strategies to help you organize your narrative:

- Introduce a narrator and/or characters.

  > Characters can be introduced all at once or throughout the narrative.

  > Choose the role each character will play.

- Establish a context.

  > Begin with your **exposition**—decide what background information your readers need to know about the characters, setting, and conflict.

  > List the events of the **rising action**—be sure that these events build toward the climax.

  > Describe what will happen during the **climax** of the story—make sure that this is the point of highest interest, conflict, or suspense in your story.

  > List the events of the **falling action**—make sure that these events show what happens to the characters as a result of the climax.

  > Explain the **resolution** of the main conflict in your story.

YOUR TURN

Complete the chart below by matching each event to its correct place in the narrative sequence.

Event Options	
A	Her parents take out a boat at dusk to go fishing. They tell her to call for help if they're not back an hour after it gets dark.
B	They find Chloe's parents sitting on some rocks, their boat having capsized.
C	Chloe, her parents, and the man all get back to their cabins safely.
D	Chloe is on vacation with her parents.
E	When her parents still haven't come back after dark, Chloe asks a man in a neighboring cabin for help. They take his boat out to look for them.

Narrative Sequence	Event
Exposition	
Rising Action	
Climax	
Falling Action	
Resolution	

YOUR TURN

Complete the chart below by writing a short summary of what will happen in each section of your narrative.

Narrative Sequence	Event
Exposition	
Rising Action	
Climax	
Falling Action	
Resolution	

Please note that excerpts and passages in the StudySync® library and this workbook are intended as touchstones to generate interest in an author's work. The excerpts and passages do not substitute for the reading of entire texts, and StudySync® strongly recommends that students seek out and purchase the whole literary or informational work in order to experience it as the author intended. Links to online resellers are available in our digital library. In addition, complete works may be ordered through an authorized reseller by filling out and returning to StudySync® the order form enclosed in this workbook.

Reading & Writing
Companion

101

Narrative Writing Process: Draft

PLAN	DRAFT	REVISE	EDIT AND PUBLISH

You have already made progress toward writing your narrative. Now it is time to draft your narrative.

✏ WRITE

Use your Plan and other responses in your Binder to draft your narrative. You may also have new ideas as you begin drafting. Feel free to explore those new ideas as they occur to you. You can also ask yourself these questions:

• Have I included specifics about my setting, characters, plot, theme, and point of view?

• Have I made the conflict in the story clear to readers?

• Does the sequence of events in my story make sense?

• Does my main character face a challenge in the story?

Before you submit your draft, read it over carefully. You want to be sure that you've responded to all aspects of the prompt.

Here is Nik's short story draft. As you read, identify details that Nik includes in his inciting incident. As Nik continues to revise and edit his narrative, he will find and improve weak spots in his writing, as well as correct any language, punctuation, or spelling mistakes.

☰ STUDENT MODEL: FIRST DRAFT

NOTES

An Unexpected Challenge

~~Tyler heard sirens. Then he smelled smoke. He wonder what was going on. He looked out the window. He saw smoke and fire trucks below. Mr. Molano was standing on the curb waveing her arms.~~

~~Tyler opened his bedroom door. "Dad?" he yelled, looking around wildly. "DAD!"~~

Even before he opened his eyes that Saturday morning, Tyler could hear the sirens. He tried to turn over and go back to sleep, but the piercing sound grew louder. Then he smelled smoke. Was his house on fire? Where were his parents? Tyler leaped out of bed and ran to the window. He gripped the windowsill tightly as he took in the scene. Smoke was pouring out of the house across the way. Three fire trucks, their lights blinking, were parked in the street. Mr. Molano stood on the curb in his pajamas, gesturing wildly.

Tyler flew to his bedroom door and flung it open. "Dad?" he yelled, looking around wildly. "DAD!"

Tyler went down the stairs. Him father was standing in the kitchen he was holding the Molanos' infant daughter, Tonya. Next to him, their 8-year-old son Max stood staring.

~~"You saw the fire? Mrs. Molano has been taken to the hospital. I think she'll be fine, but Mr. Molano is too upset to drive. I have to take him to the hospital, and I need you to watch Tonya and Max until I get back."~~

~~"I don't know how to. . ."~~

~~"I know this is a lot to ask. But you mom is at her office seeing patients until noon."~~

~~"But . . ."~~

Skill:
Story Beginnings

To engage readers in the story, Nik has them experience the fire the way Tyler does. Nik uses the action method to grab readers' attention and set an urgent tone in the first paragraph.

Skill:
Descriptive Details

Nik adds descriptive details to his draft so that readers can better imagine what is happening during this part of the story. Sound details like "the piercing sound grew louder" help readers imagine what Tyler hears in this specific event.

NOTES

Skill: Narrative Techniques

Nik decides that the reason for dialogue in this section is to advance the plot and show why the characters, Tyler and his father, are under pressure. He adds dialogue tags to make it clear who is talking.

~~"Tonya will probably sleep until we get back. I'll place her in your bed and surround her with pillows so her will be safe. See if you can get Max to eat some breakfast. Then take he up to your room so you can watch Tonya."~~

"I was just going to get you," Tyler's father said. "You saw the fire? Luckily no one has been seriously hurt. Look, I know this is a lot to ask, but I need your help here. Mrs. Molano has been taken to the hospital. I think she'll be fine, but Mr. Molano is too upset to drive. I have to take him to the hospital, and I need you to watch Tonya and Max until I get back."

Suddenly Tyler looked like *he* was in shock. "Look after *Tonya?* Dad, is she even a year old? I don't know how to . . ."

Tyler's father cut him off. "Tyler, I know this is a lot to ask. But your mom is at her office seeing patients until noon. There's no one else who can do this right now. Mr. Molano's sister is coming to see to their house, but she lives an hour away."

"But . . ."

"Tonya will probably sleep until we get back, Tyler. I'll place her in your bed and surround her with pillows so she'll be safe. See if you can get Max to eat some breakfast. Then take him up to your room so you can watch Tonya."

~~His father had gone up the stairs. Then out the door. Tyler just stood there. Slowly, he looked down at Max. "Um, would you like some breakfast, Max"? he said. The boy just nodded, and Tyler led them over to the kitchen table.~~

~~Tyler thought about making pancakes. He had watched his father make them often enough. Sometimes on Saturday mornings the whole family would sit in the kitchen and watch as Dad mixed the batter and cooked each pancake. But it would take too long. He opened a cabinet and found some cereal.~~

~~"Is this okay?"~~

~~The boy nodded again. Then, unexpectedly, he burst into tears. "Me want my mom"!~~

Almost before Tyler knew it, his father had swept up the stairs and then out the door. Tyler just stood there. Slowly, he looked down at Max. "Um, would you like some breakfast, Max?" he said. The boy just nodded, and Tyler led him over to the kitchen table.

Tyler thought about making pancakes. He had watched his father make them often enough. But it would take too long. He opened a cabinet and pulled out some cereal.

"Is this okay, Max?" Tyler asked.

The boy nodded again. Then, unexpectedly, he burst into tears. "I want my mom!" he wailed.

Tyler froze. What should she do? Then he remembered. What his father had said—Mrs. Molano would be all right.

Tyler patted the boy on the shoulder. As he poared some cereal into the bowl, he said "Don't worry, buddy. Your mom will be okay, the doctors at the hospital will take good care of them. My dad said he thought she would be fine. You'll see".

Max looked up at Tyler. He sniffed a few times. Then smiled weakly. Tyler went to get him some tissue so Max could wipe their eyes.

After Max finished his cereal, Tyler said "Let's go check on Tonya. Also, I've got a big picture book about space pirates I think you're going to like"!

Max grins and Tyler felt a flood of relief. He wasn't sure how he would deal with Max if he started crying again.

Soon Max was sitting on the floor reading. For a moment, everything was wonderfully quiet. Tyler walked over to the window and peared out. The fire seemed under control. There was no more smoke at least. Best of all, it didn't seem as if the house had been damaged very much. If it had been, Tyler wondered where the Molano would stay. Would they live in Tyler's house until their house was repaired?

Skill:
Transitions

Nik continues to add transitions throughout the rest of the story to show relationships between ideas from one paragraph to the next in his narrative. He decides to use the transitional phrase "almost before Tyler knew it" before "his father had swept up the stairs . . ." This signals a shift in time and how quickly the events are taking place.

NOTES

Then, suddenly, Tonya woke up. It was as if someone had flipped a switch. The tiny baby goes from a sound sleep to full-on crying mode. Tyler's eyes widened and he looked at Max. "What should I do"? him asked. "Mom always picks her up," Max said.

Tyler bent over and carefully picks up the baby he was terrified that he might drop her. But she still cried.

"Okay, now what?" Tyler asked.

"You should walk around with her."

Tyler walks around the bedroom and into the hallway with the baby. The motion seemed to calm her down. But anytime Tyler stopped walking Tonya began crying again. "Okay, Tonya, you the boss. I'll keep walking" Tyler said.

~~After Tyler had circled the hallway yet again, his mom came home. Tyler was so happy to see her.~~

~~"Well, look at you!" Mom said. "May I hold her?"~~

~~"You bet. Boy, my arms are tired!"~~

~~As his mother took Tonya into her arms, she said, "Great job, Tyler."~~

After Tyler had circled the hallway for what felt like the five-hundredth time, his mom came home. Tyler had never been so glad to see her in his life.

"Well, look at you!" Mom said. "You're an expert baby walker! May I hold her?"

"You bet. Boy, my arms are tired!"

As his mother scooped Tonya into her arms, she said, "Great job, Tyler. Dad called me from the hospital and told me what was going on. I got here as soon as I could, but it looks like you didn't even need my help. I'm really proud of you for rising to the challenge and helping out."

Skill:
Conclusions

Nik revises these concluding events through character dialogue between Tyler and his mom. He sums up the story with how Tyler has changed and what his mom thinks about him.

Copyright © BookheadEd Learning, LLC

"Dad and Max were the real experts," Tyler said. "I just did what them told me to do."

Tyler's mother was smiling at Max. "Your mom's going to be fine, Max," she said. "She'll be home tomorrow."

Max clapped and at the same time Tonya started crying again. Tyler's mother placed the baby in he arms.

"Here. Your the champion baby walker!"

Please note that excerpts and passages in the StudySync® library and this workbook are intended as touchstones to generate interest in an author's work. The excerpts and passages do not substitute for the reading of entire texts, and StudySync® strongly recommends that students seek out and purchase the whole literary or informational work in order to experience it as the author intended. Links to online resellers are available in our digital library. In addition, complete works may be ordered through an authorized reseller by filling out and returning to StudySync® the order form enclosed in this workbook.

Reading & Writing Companion 107

Skill:
Story Beginnings

••• CHECKLIST FOR STORY BEGINNINGS

Before you begin to write the beginning of your narrative, ask yourself the following questions:

- What kind of information does my reader need to know at the beginning of the story about the main character, the setting, and the character's conflict?

- What will happen to my character in the story?

There are many ways to engage and orient the reader to your narrative. Here are four methods to consider to help you establish a context and introduce the narrator and/or characters:

- Action

  > What action could help reveal information about my character or conflict?

  > How might an exciting moment grab my reader's attention?

  > How could a character's reaction help set the mood of my narrative?

- Description

  > Does my story take place in a special location or specific time period?

  > How can describing a location or character grab my reader's attention?

- Dialogue

  > What dialogue would help my reader understand the setting or the conflict?

  > How could a character's internal thoughts provide information for my reader?

- Information

  > Would a surprising statement grab my reader's attention?

  > What details will help my reader understand the character, conflict, or setting?

Copyright © BookheadEd Learning, LLC

YOUR TURN

Read the beginning of each story below. Then, complete the chart by writing the type of story beginning that correctly matches each paragraph.

Story Beginning Options			
Description	Action	Information	Dialogue

Story Beginning	Type of Story Beginning
Back in 1946, when I was nine, I worried that I wasn't tough enough. That's why I became a Boy Scout. Scouting, I thought, would make a man of me. It didn't take long to reach Tenderfoot rank. You got that for joining. To move up to Second Class, however, you had to meet three requirements. Scout Spirit and Scout Participation were a cinch. The third requirement, Scout Craft, meant I had to go on an overnight hike in the country. In other words, I had to leave Brooklyn, on my own, for the first time in my life. "Scout's Honor"	
"Sit down, sit down. Don't be afraid." Chairman Jin pointed to the empty chair. "These comrades from your father's work unit are just here to have a study session with you. It's nothing to worry about." *Red Scarf Girl*	
I know he's in there, I thought. I saw the curtains in his bedroom move—only a little, yes, but they moved. "The Good Samaritan"	
They would look for him, look for the plane. His father and mother would be frantic. They would tear the world apart to find him. Brian had seen searches on the news, seen movies about lost planes. When a plane went down, they mounted extensive searches and almost always they found the plane within a day or two. *Hatchet*	

✏ WRITE

Use the questions in the checklist to revise the beginning of your narrative.

Skill:
Descriptive Details

••• CHECKLIST FOR DESCRIPTIVE DETAILS

First, reread the draft of your narrative and identify the following:

- where descriptive details are needed to convey experiences and events
- vague, general, or overused words and phrases
- places where you want to tell how something looks, sounds, feels, smells, or tastes, such as:

  > experiences

  > events

Use precise words and phrases, relevant descriptive details, figurative language such as metaphors and similes, and sensory language to convey experiences and events, using the following questions as a guide:

- What experiences and events do I want to convey in my writing?
- Have I included descriptive details that are relevant and make sense in my story?
- Where can I add descriptive details to describe the characters and the events of the plot?
- Have I told how something looks, sounds, feels, smells, or tastes in order to help the reader picture the story in their mind?
- Could I use a metaphor, simile, or some other kind of figurative language to make my description more engaging?
- What can I refine or revise in my word choice to make sure that the reader can picture what is taking place?

↻ YOUR TURN

Choose the best answer to each question.

1. The following section is from an earlier draft of Nik's story. In the underlined sentence, Nik did not use the most appropriate word to describe the sound of the sirens. Which of the following is the best replacement for the word *crazy*?

> When he woke up, Tyler could hear the sirens. <u>The crazy sound grew louder and louder.</u> He could no longer go back to sleep.

- ○ A. dull
- ○ B. red
- ○ C. ear-splitting
- ○ D. large

2. Nik wants to add a descriptive sensory visual detail to this sentence from a previous draft. Which sentence BEST adds sight detail to his sentence?

> The fire looked like it was under control.

- ○ A. The bright orange flames got fainter and fainter against the bright blue sky and the fire finally looked like it was under control.
- ○ B. As Tyler took a deep breath in, the scent of smoke seemed less extreme—the fire looked like it was under control.
- ○ C. The fire looked like it was under control and Tyler could no longer hear the welcome sound of the firehose blasting the raging flames.
- ○ D. With the syrupy sweet taste of soda still circulating in his mouth, Tyler noticed that the fire finally looked like it was under control.

Please note that excerpts and passages in the StudySync® library and this workbook are intended as touchstones to generate interest in an author's work. The excerpts and passages do not substitute for the reading of entire texts, and StudySync® strongly recommends that students seek out and purchase the whole literary or informational work in order to experience it as the author intended. Links to online resellers are available in our digital library. In addition, complete works may be ordered through an authorized reseller by filling out and returning to StudySync® the order form enclosed in this workbook.

Reading & Writing Companion   **111**

YOUR TURN

Complete the chart by writing a descriptive detail that appeals to each sense for your narrative.

Sense	Descriptive Detail
sight	
smell	
touch	
taste	
sound	

Skill:
Narrative Techniques

••• CHECKLIST FOR NARRATIVE TECHNIQUES

As you begin to develop the techniques you will use in your narrative, ask yourself the following questions:

- Which characters are talking? How am I organizing the dialogue?
- How quickly or slowly do I want the plot to move? Why?
- Which literary devices can be added to strengthen the characters or plot? How can I better engage the reader?

There are many techniques you can use in a narrative. Here are some methods that can help you write dialogue, pacing, and description, to develop experiences, events, and/or characters:

- Use dialogue between characters to explain events or move the action forward.

  > Set all dialogue off in quotation marks.

  > Include identifying names as needed before or after quotation marks.

- Include description to engage the reader and help them visualize the characters, setting, and other elements in the narrative.

  > Include only those descriptions relevant to the reader's understanding of the element being described.

- Use pacing effectively to convey a sense of urgency or calm in a narrative.

  > To speed up the pace, try using limited description, short paragraphs, brief dialogue, and simpler sentences.

  > To slow down the pace, try using detailed description, longer paragraphs, and more complex sentence structures.

- Use any combination of the above narrative techniques to develop experiences, events, and/or characters.

↻ YOUR TURN

Choose the best answer to each question.

1. The following section is from a previous draft of Nik's story. What change, if any, needs to be made in the underlined sentence?

> Before Tyler knew it, his father had run up the stairs and out the door. Tyler stood there nervously and then looked down at Max. <u>Um, would you like me to refill your water bottle, Max?" he said.</u> The boy nodded, so Tyler walked him over to the sink.

○ A. Change *your* to *you're*.
○ B. Insert quotation marks at the beginning of the sentence.
○ C. Change *said* to *says*.
○ D. The underlined sentence does not need to be changed.

2. The following section is from a previous draft of Nik's story. Which of the following is a description of how Tyler feels?

> Before Tyler knew it, his father had run up the stairs and out the door. Tyler stood there nervously and then looked down at Max. Um, would you like me to refill your water bottle, Max?" he said. The boy nodded, so Tyler walked him over to the sink.

○ A. "looked down at Max"
○ B. "walked him over to the sink"
○ C. "stood there nervously"
○ D. "before Tyler knew it"

3. The following sentences are from a previous draft of Nik's story. What is the correct way to write the sentences?

> "The real experts are Dad and Max," Tyler said. "I just did what I was asked."

○ A. The real experts are Dad and Max," Tyler said. "I just did what I was asked."

○ B. "The real experts are Dad and Max," Tyler said. I just did what I was asked."

○ C. "The real experts are Dad and Max, Tyler said. I just did what I was asked."

○ D. The sentences are written correctly in the story.

 WRITE

Use the questions in the checklist to add narrative techniques, such as writing new dialogue, for your narrative.

Please note that excerpts and passages in the StudySync® library and this workbook are intended as touchstones to generate interest in an author's work. The excerpts and passages do not substitute for the reading of entire texts, and StudySync® strongly recommends that students seek out and purchase the whole literary or informational work in order to experience it as the author intended. Links to online resellers are available in our digital library. In addition, complete works may be ordered through an authorized reseller by filling out and returning to StudySync® the order form enclosed in this workbook.

Reading & Writing Companion 115

Skill:
Transitions

••• CHECKLIST FOR TRANSITIONS

Before you revise your current draft to include transitions, think about:

- the order of events including the rising action, climax, falling action, and resolution
- moments where the time or setting changes

Next, reread your current draft and note areas in your story where:

- the order of events is unclear or illogical
- when changes in time or setting are confusing or unclear. Look for:

  > sudden jumps in time and setting

  > missing or illogical plot events

  > places where you could add more context or exposition, such as important background information about the narrator, setting, characters, and conflict, to help the reader understand where and when plot events are happening

Revise your draft to use a variety of transition words, phrases, and clauses to convey sequence and signal shifts from one time frame or setting to another, using the following questions as a guide:

- Does my exposition provide necessary background information?
- Do the events of the rising action, climax, falling action, and resolution flow naturally and logically?
- Did I include a variety of transition words and phrases that show sequence and signal setting and time changes?

  > transitions such as *that night* or *on the first sunny day* can indicate changes in time periods

  > phrases such as *a week later, Bob boarded a train to Iowa* can indicate shifts in setting and time

⟳ YOUR TURN

Choose the best answer to each question.

1. Which of the following is a transition word that signals a shift in time in this sentence?

> After Max finished his cereal, Tyler said, "Let's go check on Tonya. Also, I've got a big picture book about space pirates I think you're going to like!"

○ A. "After"
○ B. "check"
○ C. "Also"
○ D. "finished"

2. Which of the following phrases includes transition words that signal a shift in action?

> Then, suddenly, Tonya woke up. It was as if someone had flipped a switch. The tiny baby went from a sound sleep to full-on crying mode. Tyler's eyes widened and he looked at Max. "What should I do?" he asked.

○ A. "as if someone had flipped a switch"
○ B. "from a sound sleep"
○ C. "Then, suddenly"
○ D. "Tyler's eyes widened."

⟳ YOUR TURN

Complete the chart by adding transitions that organize the structure of your draft and show the relationship between ideas.

Transitions that organize the story structure	Transitions that show the relationship between ideas

Skill:
Conclusions

••• CHECKLIST FOR CONCLUSIONS

Before you write your conclusion, ask yourself the following questions:

- What important details should I include in the summary in my conclusion?
- What other thoughts and feelings could the characters share with readers in the conclusion?
- Should I express the importance of the events in my narrative through dialogue or a character's actions?

Below are two strategies to help you provide a conclusion that follows from the narrated experiences or events:

- Peer Discussion

    > After you have written your introduction and body paragraphs, talk with a partner about possible endings for your narrative, writing notes about your discussion.

    > Review your notes and think about how you want to end your story.

    > Briefly summarize the events in the narrative through the narrator or one of the characters.

    > Describe how the narrator feels about the events they experienced.

    > Reveal to readers why the experiences in the narrative matter through a character's reflections or dialogue.

    > Write your conclusion.

- Freewriting

    > Freewrite for 10 minutes about what you might include in your conclusion. Don't worry about grammar, punctuation, or having fully formed ideas. The point of freewriting is to discover ideas.

    > Review your notes and think about how you want to end your story.

    > Briefly summarize the events in the narrative through the narrator or one of the characters.

    > Describe how the narrator feels about the events they experienced.

    > Reveal to readers why the experiences in the narrative matter through a character's reflections or dialogue.

    > Write your conclusion.

YOUR TURN

Read the conclusions below. Then, complete the chart by sorting them into those that are strong conclusions and those that are not.

	Conclusion Options
A	"You're the champion baby walker!"
B	As his mother scooped Tonya into her arms, she said, "Great job, Tyler. Dad called me from the hospital and told me what was going on. I got here as soon as I could, but it looks like you didn't even need my help. I'm really proud of you for rising to the challenge and helping out."
C	Max clapped and at the same time Tonya started crying again.
D	But anytime Tyler stopped walking, Tonya began crying again.

Strong Conclusion	Not Strong Conclusion

✏ WRITE

Use the questions in the checklist to add a conclusion: use details, dialogue, action, and character feelings or thoughts to conclude your narrative.

Narrative Writing Process: Revise

PLAN	DRAFT	REVISE	EDIT AND PUBLISH

You have written a draft of your narrative. You have also received input from your peers about how to improve it. Now you are going to revise your draft.

◀◀ REVISION GUIDE

Examine your draft to find areas for revision. Keep in mind your purpose and audience as you revise for clarity, development, organization, and style. Use the guide below to help you review.

Review	Revise	Example
Clarity		
Label each piece of dialogue so you know who is speaking. Annotate any places where it is unclear who is speaking.	Use the character's name to show who is speaking or add description about the speaker.	"Is this okay, Max?" Tyler asked. The boy nodded again. Then, unexpectedly, he burst into tears. "I want my mom!" he wailed.
Development		
Identify key moments leading up to the climax. Annotate places that don't move the story along toward the climax or the resolution.	Focus on a single event and think carefully about whether it drives the story forward or keeps it standing still. If it doesn't move the story forward, you might consider adding or subtracting details to make it more important to the plot.	Tyler thought about making pancakes. He had watched his father make them often enough. ~~Sometimes on Saturday mornings the whole family would sit in the kitchen and keep Dad company while he mixed the batter and cooked each pancake.~~ But it would take too long. He opened a cabinet and pulled out some cereal.

Review	Revise	Example
Organization		
Explain your story in one or two sentences. Reread and annotate any parts that don't match your explanation.	Rewrite the events in the correct sequence. Delete events that are not essential to the story.	Soon Max was sitting on the floor reading. For a moment, everything was wonderfully quiet. Tyler walked over to the window and peered out. The fire seemed under control. There was no more smoke at least. Best of all, it didn't seem as if the house had been damaged very much. ~~If it had been, Tyler wondered where the Molanos would stay. Would they live in Tyler's house until their house was repaired?~~
Style: Word Choice		
Identify every pronoun that takes the place of a noun in your story.	Select sentences to rewrite using consistent pronoun use and correct pronoun and antecedent agreement.	Mr. Molano was standing on the curb waving ~~her~~ his arms.
Style: Sentence Variety		
Think about a key event where you want your reader to feel a specific emotion. Long sentences can draw out a moment and make a reader think; short sentences can show urgent actions or danger.	Rewrite a key event making your sentences longer or shorter to achieve the emotion you want your reader to feel.	After Tyler had circled the hallway ~~yet again,~~ for what felt like the five-hundredth time, his mom came home. Tyler ~~was so happy to see her~~ had never been so glad to see her in his life.

WRITE

Use the guide above, as well as your peer reviews, to help you evaluate your narrative to determine areas that should be revised.

Grammar:
Personal Pronouns

Personal pronouns are pronouns used to refer to persons or things. Two cases, or forms, that pronouns take are nominative case, or subject, and objective case, or object. Each case is determined by how the pronoun functions in a sentence.

Subject Pronouns:
Singular: *I, you, he, she, it*
Plural: *we, you, they*

Object Pronouns:
Singular: *me, you, him, her*
Plural: *us, you, them*

They might come today. Hatchet	The subject pronoun *they* is the subject of the sentence.
In this manner, stopping to rest when I was tired, I carried **him** to the headland. Island of the Blue Dolphins	The object pronoun *him* is the object of the verb *carried*.
There were threats against **me** and my family and even out-and-out attempts at physical harm to **me**. I Never Had It Made: An Autobiography of Jackie Robinson	The object pronoun *me* is the object of the prepositions *against* and *to*.

When writing, make sure to use pronouns in the correct case.

Correct	Incorrect
I walk one mile to school every day.	Me walk one mile to school every day.
Paula asked them for help.	Paula asked they for help.

Copyright © BookheadEd Learning, LLC

↻ YOUR TURN

1. How should this sentence be changed?

   > Them mow lawns during summer vacation.

   ○ A. Change **Them** to **Her**.
   ○ B. Change **Them** to **They**.
   ○ C. Change **Them** to **Him**.
   ○ D. No change needs to be made to this sentence.

2. How should this sentence be changed?

   > She told he a funny joke.

   ○ A. Change **he** to **him**.
   ○ B. Change **she** to **her**.
   ○ C. Change **he** to **they**.
   ○ D. No change needs to be made to this sentence.

3. How should this sentence be changed?

   > We nervously watched the big, brown dog approach us.

   ○ A. Change **We** to **Us**.
   ○ B. Change **We** to **Him**.
   ○ C. Change **us** to **we**.
   ○ D. No change needs to be made to this sentence.

4. How should this sentence be changed?

   > Her brought Cara for a visit.

   ○ A. Change **Cara** to **she**.
   ○ B. Change **Her** to **Us**.
   ○ C. Change **Her** to **She**.
   ○ D. No change needs to be made to this sentence.

Grammar:
Pronouns and Antecedents

Pronouns and Antecedents

A pronoun is a word that takes the place of a noun mentioned earlier. The noun is the pronoun's antecedent. A pronoun must agree in number and gender with its antecedent.

Text	Pronoun	Antecedent
The morning after my **teacher** came she led me into **her** room and gave me a doll. The Story of My Life	her	teacher
Some of the **Dodgers** who swore **they** would never play with a black man had a change of mind, when **they** realized I was a good ballplayer who could be helpful in **their** earning a few thousand more dollars in world series money. I Never Had It Made: An Autobiography of Jackie Robinson	they their	Dodgers
On this bus on that day, **Rosa Parks** initiated a new era in the American quest for freedom and equality. **She** sat near the middle of the bus, just behind the 10 seats reserved for whites. The Story Behind the Bus	she	Rosa Parks

A pronoun's antecedent should always be clear.

Clear	Unclear	Explanation
Andrea and her sister baked bread. **Her sister** had a special talent for it.	Andrea and her sister baked bread. **She** had a special talent for it.	The pronoun *she* in the second sentence could refer to either Andrea or her sister.
The diplomats, who had traveled from Puerto Rico, met with the reporters.	The diplomats met with the reporters. **They** had traveled from Puerto Rico.	The pronoun *they* could refer to either the diplomats or the reporters.

↻ YOUR TURN

1. How should this sentence be changed?

> My brother has a test tomorrow, so it is going to study after dinner.

- ○ A. Change the word **it** to **we**.
- ○ B. Change the word **it** to **he**.
- ○ C. Change the word **it** to **she**.
- ○ D. No change needs to be made to this sentence.

2. How should this sentence be changed?

> John Adams disagreed with Thomas Jefferson, but he later changed his opinions.

- ○ A. Change **he** to **Adams**.
- ○ B. Change **he** to **they**.
- ○ C. Change **he** to **it**.
- ○ D. No change needs to be made to this sentence.

3. How should these sentences be changed?

> The Sistine Chapel is in Rome. Michelangelo painted it.

- ○ A. Change **Michelangelo** to **He**.
- ○ B. Change **The Sistine Chapel** to **It**.
- ○ C. Change **it** to **her**.
- ○ D. No changes need to be made to these sentences.

4. How should this sentence be changed?

> All of the teams promote its star players.

- ○ A. Change **teams** to **team**.
- ○ B. Change **its** to **their**.
- ○ C. Change **its** to **his**.
- ○ D. No change needs to be made to this sentence.

Please note that excerpts and passages in the StudySync® library and this workbook are intended as touchstones to generate interest in an author's work. The excerpts and passages do not substitute for the reading of entire texts, and StudySync® strongly recommends that students seek out and purchase the whole literary or informational work in order to experience it as the author intended. Links to online resellers are available in our digital library. In addition, complete works may be ordered through an authorized reseller by filling out and returning to StudySync® the order form enclosed in this workbook.

Reading & Writing
Companion

125

Grammar:
Consistent Pronoun Use

An antecedent is the word or group of words to which a pronoun refers or that a pronoun replaces. A pronoun must agree with its antecedent in number (singular or plural) and gender (masculine, feminine, or neutral). A pronoun's antecedent may be a noun, another pronoun, or a phrase or clause acting as a noun.

Text	Explanation
I even move **my** chair a little to the right. Not **mine**, not **mine**, not **mine**. Eleven	The pronoun *I* is the antecedent of the pronouns *my* and *mine*. The pronouns agree in person and number.
"Oh, I forgot to show you my pigs!" **he** exclaimed, the gleam returning to **his** eyes. The Pigman	The pronoun *he* is the antecedent of the pronoun *his*. The pronouns agree in person and number.

Pronouns should be used with consistency, so avoid shifting pronoun number and person within a sentence or passage.

Correct	Incorrect
Many older Americans know the exact date **they** started their first job.	Many older Americans know the exact date it started their first job.
My friends and I attended the football game; then **we** walked uptown.	My friends and I attended the football game; then he walked uptown.

Do not use *you* and *they* as indefinite pronouns, and avoid pronouns with no clear antecedent. If clearer, name the person or group to which you are referring.

Correct	Incorrect
As the old adage says: Better safe than sorry.	You know what they say: Better safe than sorry.
People in the community like to attend weekly basketball games. Anybody can have a great time.	People in the community like to attend weekly games. You don't have to love basketball to have a great time.

↻ YOUR TURN

1. How should this sentence be changed?

> Penelope likes the game of soccer; it plays often.

- ○ A. Change **it** to **they**.
- ○ B. Change **it** to **he**.
- ○ C. Change **it** to **she**.
- ○ D. No change needs to be made to this sentence.

2. How should this sentence be changed?

> Maria and Sean thought the computer was just what he needed to make their business work.

- ○ A. Change **he** to **they**.
- ○ B. Change **he** to **she**.
- ○ C. Change **he** to **it**.
- ○ D. No change needs to be made to this sentence.

3. How should this sentence be changed?

> Jason was spending the week with his dad in Boston, where you were going to watch two Celtics games.

- ○ A. Change **his** to **its**.
- ○ B. Change **you** to **they**.
- ○ C. Change **you** to **he**.
- ○ D. No change needs to be made to this sentence.

4. How should this sentence be changed?

> Sidney moved to the city of Seattle and became a member of its city council.

- ○ A. Change **its** to **your**.
- ○ B. Change **its** to **their**.
- ○ C. Change **its** to **our**.
- ○ D. No change needs to be made to this sentence.

Please note that excerpts and passages in the StudySync® library and this workbook are intended as touchstones to generate interest in an author's work. The excerpts and passages do not substitute for the reading of entire texts, and StudySync® strongly recommends that students seek out and purchase the whole literary or informational work in order to experience it as the author intended. Links to online resellers are available in our digital library. In addition, complete works may be ordered through an authorized reseller by filling out and returning to StudySync® the order form enclosed in this workbook.

Reading & Writing Companion   **127**

Narrative Writing Process: Edit and Publish

| PLAN | DRAFT | REVISE | EDIT AND PUBLISH |

You have revised your narrative based on your peer feedback and your own examination.

Now, it is time to edit your narrative. When you revised, you focused on the content of your narrative. You probably looked at the story's beginning, descriptive details, and dialogue. When you edit, you focus on the mechanics of your story, paying close attention to things like grammar and punctuation.

Use the checklist below to guide you as you edit:

☐ Have I followed all the rules for punctuating dialogue?

☐ Have I used correct pronoun and antecedent agreement throughout the story?

☐ Have I used correct and consistent pronouns throughout the story?

☐ Do I have any sentence fragments or run-on sentences?

☐ Have I spelled everything correctly?

Notice some edits Nik has made:

• Changed a pronoun to agree with the antecedent.

• Fixed a sentence fragment.

• Corrected spelling.

• Added a comma before a piece of dialogue.

• Fixed a run-on sentence.

• Changed a pronoun to maintain consistency.

• Moved a period inside quotation marks.

Tyler froze. What should ~~she~~ he do? Then he ~~remembered. What~~ remembered what his father had said—Mrs. Molano would be all right.

Tyler patted the boy on the shoulder. As he ~~poared~~ poured some cereal into the bowl, he ~~said "Don't~~ said, "Don't worry, buddy. Your mom will be ~~okay the~~ okay. The doctors at the hospital will take good care of ~~them~~ her. My dad said he thought she would be fine. You'll ~~see".~~ see."

✎ WRITE

Use the questions on the previous page, as well as your peer reviews, to help you evaluate your narrative to determine areas that need editing. Then edit your narrative to correct those errors.

Once you have made all your corrections, you are ready to publish your work. You can distribute your writing to family and friends, hang it on a bulletin board, or post it on your blog. If you publish online, share the link with your family, friends, and classmates.

Lost Island

FICTION

Introduction

Mariana wakes up alone, thirsty, and hungry on a deserted island. How did she get here, and why is her head throbbing? As she slowly recalls a large wave smashing into Uncle Merlin's fishing boat, Mariana takes her first steps

V VOCABULARY

damp

wet

capsized

tipped over in the water

intense

very strong

rescuer

someone who saves a person from harm or danger

anchored

held in place firmly

cautioned

gave a warning

≡ READ

NOTES

1 Mariana woke up slowly.

2 She was on her back. She felt sand in her mouth. The air was hot and **damp**. Where am I? Her head was throbbing. Was that the smell of salt in the air? Did I hear a seagull cry?

3 Mariana turned her head and slowly opened her eyes. The bright light was too **intense** for her. At first, she saw only damp yellow sand. She looked around. She saw stones, weeds, and a few palm trees. She could see the entire island. It was no larger than a soccer field.

4 Then Mariana remembered. She remembered fishing with Uncle Merlin. They found a good spot, so they **anchored** their boat near a little island. In the warm morning sun, the bay was calm. Mariana and Merlin got their fishing lines ready, when suddenly an enormous, thundering wave came out of nowhere. The wave overturned the boat, tossing them into the water. Mariana

remembered rising to the surface and seeing land. She swam toward it; she swam and swam. An eternity seemed to have passed. She remembered thinking: Why don't I just give up? What had motivated her to keep swimming? She had finally reached the shore and had crawled up onto the sand. Exhausted.

5   Mariana looked at her surroundings now and thought. She must have passed out and slept on the beach for hours. The boat had **capsized** in early morning, but now the sun was high in the sky. It must be noon.

6   Noon, and hot.

7   Mariana wondered where her uncle was. Why hasn't he come to get me? What is he waiting for? She felt hungry; her mouth was dry. She thought of the lunch her uncle had packed. A cool drink and a sandwich would be perfect right now!

8   Then she realized something. Maybe her uncle wasn't coming to get her because maybe he had drowned. Maybe no **rescuer** was coming to get her. She was trapped. Stuck. Alone. Was she going to die on this island?

9   Mariana started to cry, but she stopped herself quickly. Wait. She **cautioned** herself. Don't be a baby. Use your head. That's what Uncle Merlin always said: "Use your head!"

10 Slowly turning her body, she then lifted herself onto her elbows. Next, she got onto her knees and finally stood up. Her head throbbed, but she looked into the island and took a step.

First Read

Read the story. After you read, answer the Think Questions below.

☁ **THINK QUESTIONS**

1. Who is the main character in the story? Where is she?

   _____ is the main character.

   She is _____.

2. What happened that tipped the boat over?

   The boat tipped over because _____.

3. How can you tell that Mariana is getting more worried as time passes?

   Mariana is getting more worried because _____

   _____.

4. Use context to confirm the meaning of the word *rescuer* as it is used in "Lost Island." Write your definition of *rescuer* here.

   Rescuer means _____

   A context clue is _____.

5. What is another way to say that a boat *capsized*?

   A boat _____.

Skill:
Analyzing Expressions

★ DEFINE

When you read, you may find English **expressions** that you do not know. An expression is a group of words that communicates an idea. Three types of expressions are idioms, sayings, and figurative language. They can be difficult to understand because the meanings of the words are different from their **literal**, or usual, meanings.

An **idiom** is an expression that is commonly known among a group of people. For example: "It's raining cats and dogs" means it is raining heavily. **Sayings** are short expressions that contain advice or wisdom. For instance: "Don't count your chickens before they hatch" means do not plan on something good happening before it happens. **Figurative** language is when you describe something by comparing it with something else, either directly (using the words *like* or *as*) or indirectly. For example, "I'm as hungry as a horse" means I'm very hungry. None of the expressions are about actual animals.

••• CHECKLIST FOR ANALYZING EXPRESSIONS

To determine the meaning of an expression, remember the following:

✓ If you find a confusing group of words, it may be an expression. The meaning of words in expressions may not be their literal meaning.

- Ask yourself: Is this confusing because the words are new? Or because the words do not make sense together?

✓ Determining the overall meaning may require that you use one or more of the following:

- context clues

- a dictionary or other resource

- teacher or peer support

✓ Highlight important information before and after the expression to look for clues.

↻ YOUR TURN

Read paragraphs 9–10 from "Lost Island." Then complete the multiple-choice questions below.

---

from **"Lost Island"**

Mariana started to cry, but she stopped herself quickly. Wait. She cautioned herself. Don't be a baby. Use your head. That's what Uncle Merlin always said: "Use your head!"

Slowly turning her body, she then lifted herself onto her elbows. Next, she got onto her knees and finally stood up. Her head throbbed, but she looked into the island and took a step.

---

1. What does Mariana mean when she says "use your head" in paragraph 9?

    ○ A. find her uncle

    ○ B. to be cautious exploring

    ○ C. to use her head as a tool

    ○ D. to think about a solution

2. Which context clue helped you determine the meaning of the expression?

    ○ A. "Mariana started to cry . . ."

    ○ B. "That's what Uncle Merlin always said."

    ○ C. "Slowly turning her body . . ."

    ○ D. ". . . she got onto her knees and finally stood up."

Please note that excerpts and passages in the StudySync® library and this workbook are intended as touchstones to generate interest in an author's work. The excerpts and passages do not substitute for the reading of entire texts, and StudySync® strongly recommends that students seek out and purchase the whole literary or informational work in order to experience it as the author intended. Links to online resellers are available in our digital library. In addition, complete works may be ordered through an authorized reseller by filling out and returning to StudySync® the order form enclosed in this workbook.

Reading & Writing Companion   135

Skill:
Conveying Ideas

★ DEFINE

Conveying ideas means communicating a **message** to another person. When speaking, you might not know what word to use to convey your ideas. When you do not know the exact English word, you can try different strategies. For example, you can ask for help from classmates or your teacher. You may use gestures and physical movements to act out the word. You can also try using **synonyms** or **defining** and describing the meaning you are trying to express.

••• CHECKLIST FOR CONVEYING IDEAS

To convey ideas for words you do not know, try the following strategies:

- ✓ Request help.

- ✓ Use gestures or physical movements.

- ✓ Use a synonym for the word.

- ✓ Describe what the word means using other words.

- ✓ Give an example of the word you want to use.

⟳ YOUR TURN

Read the following excerpt from the story. Then imagine that someone is trying to convey the idea of the boat *overturning*. Find the correct example for each strategy to complete the chart below.

---

from "**Lost Island**"

Then Mariana remembered. She remembered fishing with Uncle Merlin. They found a good spot, so they anchored their boat near a little island. In the warm morning sun, the bay was calm. Mariana and Merlin got their fishing lines ready, when suddenly an enormous, thundering wave came out of nowhere. The wave overturned the boat, tossing them into the water. Mariana remembered rising to the surface and seeing land.

Examples	
A	The person explains that the word means "to roll over."
B	The person turns her or his hand upside-down.
C	The person uses the similar words *tip* over.
D	The person says this when you knock a glass over and it spills.

Strategies	Examples
Use gestures or physical movements.	
Use a synonym for the word.	
Describe what the word means using other words.	
Give examples of when you would use the word.	

Close Read

✏ WRITE

PERSONAL RESPONSE: Mariana faces dangers that few people her age ever see. How would you react if you were faced with the same situation? How would your response be like Mariana's? How would it be different? Recount the events that Mariana experienced, and describe what you might feel and do in her situation. Pay attention to spelling patterns as you write.

Use the checklist below to guide you as you write:

☐ What happens to Mariana in the story?

☐ What dangers does Mariana face?

☐ How does she act and feel?

☐ How would I be like Mariana?

☐ How would I be different from Mariana?

Use the sentence frames to organize and write your personal response.

If I were Mariana, _____ .

First, I would _____ .

Like Mariana, I would _____ .

Unlike Mariana, I might _____ .

Connected

FICTION

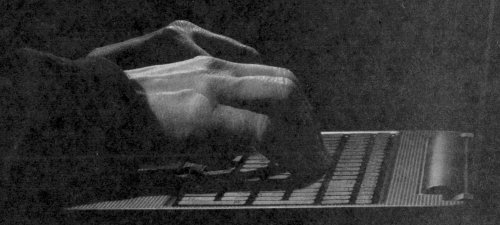

Introduction

W hat would you do if a friend went missing? What if you learned that a powerful, maybe even scary, secret lay behind the disappearance? In the story "Connected," three friends search for a missing person—and learn of a tantalizing force that could threaten the world as they know it.

V VOCABULARY

habitually
done regularly or often

digits
symbols for the numbers 0 to 9

froze
stopped in a position and without further movement

whirlpool
a place in a body of water, such as a river or a stream, where the water moves very fast in a circle

virus
a software program that is created to cause harm to a computer or network

NOTES

≡ READ

1 Joshua was late. At first, his friends were not surprised. Joshua was **habitually** late. Joshua liked to stay connected to the Internet. His friends thought he was *too* connected.

2 But it was opening night for the biggest movie of the summer. Joshua should have met them hours ago.

3 "Did you hear from him today?" Victoria asked. Ibrahim and Mateo shook their heads.

4 She frowned. "Something's not right. We need to see what's going on."

5 "I know where he could be," Ibrahim said.

6 "His computer," they all exclaimed.

. . .

7   Ibrahim opened the door to Joshua's room and **froze**. Clothes, food wrappers, and comic books were on the floor. A blue light glowed on Joshua's computer. He wasn't there.

8   "Start looking," Victoria said.

9   "For what?" Ibrahim asked.

10 "I don't know," Victoria answered, "but I think we'll find a clue."

11 Mateo stood behind his friends.

12 Ibrahim searched Joshua's backpack. Victoria checked some notebooks. She saw Mateo's eyes before he glanced down.

13 "What's wrong? Aren't you going to help us?"

14 Mateo mumbled something but didn't look up.

15 "What is it?" Ibrahim asked.

16 Mateo answered, "A few days ago Joshua told me he discovered a **virus**. He said it was different. It could take over any computer."

17 "But there was more," Mateo continued. "Joshua said the virus could take over *anyone*. He was going to find out who created it. He asked me not to tell."

18 Victoria and Ibrahim were shocked. Mateo stepped forward.

19 "What about his computer?" he asked. "Maybe he left something there."

20 "Yes!" said Victoria.

21 The three friends gathered around the computer. Ibrahim took the mouse and clicked.

22 They saw white numbers moving across the screen. Soon, the **digits** moved faster. First, they moved diagonally, like rippling water. Then, they moved in circles like a **whirlpool**. The three friends moved closer to the screen. They couldn't look away. The numbers blurred and four words appeared:

23   *Enter, if you wish*

24 Ibrahim pressed [Enter].

25 They saw a bright flash and had to close their eyes. When they opened their eyes, they were in a long hallway.

26 They could see a shape. It was the figure of a man, moving toward them.

27 "That was an interesting choice, wouldn't you say?" the figure said coolly. The words hung in the air like icicles.

28 Victoria spoke first. "Who are you?" she asked, her voice shivering.

29 "We will get to that. And we will get to your friend. But first you must do something for us."

First Read

Read the story. After you read, answer the Think Questions below.

1. What is Joshua late for at the beginning of the story?

    Joshua is late for _____.

2. Where did Joshua's friends go to find him? What did they find?

    Joshua's friends went to _____.

    They found _____.

3. What happened when Ibrahim pressed [Enter] on the computer?

    There was _____.

4. Use context to confirm the meaning of the word *habitually* as it is used in "Connected." Write your definition of *habitually* here.

    Habitually means _____.

    A context clue is _____.

5. What is another way to say that Ibrahim *froze*?

    Ibrahim was _____.

Please note that excerpts and passages in the StudySync® library and this workbook are intended as touchstones to generate interest in an author's work. The excerpts and passages do not substitute for the reading of entire texts, and StudySync® strongly recommends that students seek out and purchase the whole literary or informational work in order to experience it as the author intended. Links to online resellers are available in our digital library. In addition, complete works may be ordered through an authorized reseller by filling out and returning to StudySync® the order form enclosed in this workbook.

Reading & Writing Companion **143**

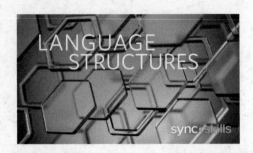

Skill:
Language Structures

 DEFINE

In every language, there are rules that tell how to **structure** sentences. These rules define the correct order of words. In the English language, for example, a **basic** structure for sentences is subject, verb, and object. Some sentences have more **complicated** structures.

You will encounter both basic and complicated **language structures** in the classroom materials you read. Being familiar with language structures will help you better understand the text.

••• CHECKLIST FOR LANGUAGE STRUCTURES

To improve your comprehension of language structures, do the following:

✓ Monitor your understanding.

- Ask yourself: Why do I not understand this sentence? Is it because I do not understand some of the words? Or is it because I do not understand the way the words are ordered in the sentence?

✓ Break down the sentence into its parts.

✓ In English, most sentences share the same pattern: subject + verb + object.

- The **subject** names who or what is doing the action.
- The **verb** names the action or state of being.
- The **object** answers questions such as "Who?," "What?," "Where?," and "When?"

✓ Ask yourself: What is the subject and the verb of this sentence? What details do the other words provide?

✓ Confirm your understanding with a peer or teacher.

YOUR TURN

Read the following excerpt from "Connected." Then, complete the chart by writing the words and phrases into the "Subject," "Verb," and "Object" columns. The first row has been done as an example.

---

from **"Connected"**

Mateo stood behind his friends.

Ibrahim searched Joshua's backpack. Victoria checked some notebooks. She saw Mateo's eyes before he glanced down.

Sentence	Subject	Verb	Object
Mateo stood behind his friends.	Mateo	stood	behind his friends
Ibrahim searched Joshua's backpack.			
Victoria checked some notebooks.			
She saw Mateo's eyes before he glanced down.			

Please note that excerpts and passages in the StudySync® library and this workbook are intended as touchstones to generate interest in an author's work. The excerpts and passages do not substitute for the reading of entire texts, and StudySync® strongly recommends that students seek out and purchase the whole literary or informational work in order to experience it as the author intended. Links to online resellers are available in our digital library. In addition, complete works may be ordered through an authorized reseller by filling out and returning to StudySync® the order form enclosed in this workbook.

Reading & Writing Companion   **145**

Skill: Retelling and Summarizing

★ DEFINE

You can retell and summarize a text after reading to show your understanding. **Retelling** is telling a story again in your own words. **Summarizing** is giving a short explanation of the most important ideas in a text.

Keep your retelling or summary **concise**. Only include important information and keywords from the text. By summarizing and retelling a text, you can improve your comprehension of the text's ideas.

••• CHECKLIST FOR RETELLING AND SUMMARIZING

In order to retell or summarize text, note the following:

✓ Identify the main events of the text.

- Ask yourself: What happens in this text? What are the main events that happen at the beginning, the middle, and the end of the text?

✓ Identify the main ideas in a text.

- Ask yourself: What are the most important ideas in the text?

✓ Determine the answers to the 6 *Wh-* questions.

- Ask yourself: After reading this text, can I answer Who? What? Where? When? Why? and How? questions.

↻ YOUR TURN

Read the following excerpt from "Connected." Then, write the events in the beginning, middle, and end of the excerpt to retell what happened.

---

from "Connected"

They saw white numbers moving across the screen. Soon, the digits moved faster. First, they moved diagonally, like rippling water. Then, they moved in circles like a whirlpool. The three friends moved closer to the screen. They couldn't look away. The numbers blurred and four words appeared: *Enter, if you wish.*

Event Options		
The friends moved closer to the screen.	The words "Enter, if you wish" appeared on the screen.	They saw numbers moving across the screen.

Beginning	
Middle	
End	

Close Read

 WRITE

PERSONAL RESPONSE: Would you have pressed [Enter] like Joshua's friends did? Write a short paragraph that explains your reasoning. Support your explanation with details and evidence from the text. Pay attention to subject-verb agreement as you write.

Use the checklist below to guide you as you write.

☐ What happened at the beginning and middle of the story?

☐ Why did Joshua's friends press [Enter] at the end of the story?

☐ What would you have done that is the same?

☐ What would you have done that is different?

Use the sentence frames to organize and write your personal response.

In the beginning, Joshua's friends realized that Joshua was _____.

They went to his room to look for _____.

Matteo remembered Joshua talking about a _____.

The friends decided to look at Joshua's _____.

Like Joshua's friends, I would have _____

because _____.

However, I would not have _____

because _____.

PHOTO/IMAGE CREDITS:

Text Fulfillment
Through StudySync

If you are interested in specific titles, please fill out the form below and we will check availability through our partners.

ORDER DETAILS

Date:

TITLE	AUTHOR	Paperback/ Hardcover	Specific Edition *If Applicable*	Quantity

SHIPPING INFORMATION	BILLING INFORMATION ☐ *SAME AS SHIPPING*
Contact:	Contact:
Title:	Title:
School/District:	School/District:
Address Line 1:	Address Line 1:
Address Line 2:	Address Line 2:
Zip or Postal Code:	Zip or Postal Code:
Phone:	Phone:
Mobile:	Mobile:
Email:	Email:

PAYMENT INFORMATION

☐ CREDIT CARD   Name on Card:

Card Number: Expiration Date: Security Code:

☐ PO   Purchase Order Number:

StudySync Text Fulfillment, BookheadEd Learning, LLC
610 Daniel Young Drive | Sonoma, CA 95476